From JavaScript to TypeScript: Navigating the Modern Web Transition

Kameron Hussain and Frahaan Hussain

Published by Sonar Publishing, 2023.

While every precaution has been taken in the preparation of this book, the publisher assumes no responsibility for errors or omissions, or for damages resulting from the use of the information contained herein.

FROM JAVASCRIPT TO TYPESCRIPT: NAVIGATING THE MODERN WEB TRANSITION

First edition. November 30, 2023.

Copyright © 2023 Kameron Hussain and Frahaan Hussain.

ISBN: 979-8223745853

Written by Kameron Hussain and Frahaan Hussain.

Table of Contents

Chapter 2: TypeScript Basics

2.1 Understanding TypeScript Syntax

Variable Declarations

Data Types

Type Inference

Type Annotations

Basic Control Flow

Functions

2. Code Splitting

3. Lazy Loading

4. Tree Shaking

5. Module Resolution Strategies

10.4 TypeScript in Microservices Architecture

1. Service Independence

2. Communication between Microservices

3. Scaling and Deployment

4. Testing and Integration

5. Monitoring and Logging

6. Service Discovery and Load Balancing

10.5 Managing Dependencies in Large Projects

1. Use Dependency Management Tools

2. Semantic Versioning

3. Lock Files

4. Organize Dependencies

5. Use TypeScript's Type Definitions

6. Dependency Auditing

7. Use Dependency Injection

8. Continuous Integration and Deployment (CI/CD)

6. Avoid Excessive Cloning:

7. Memory Considerations in Asynchronous Code:

Section 11.5: Tips for Efficient TypeScript Coding

1. Consistent Coding Style:

2. Use TypeScript's Type System Effectively:

3. Destructuring and Object Spreading:

4. Avoid Excessive Nesting:

5. Error Handling:

6. Asynchronous Programming:

7. Code Splitting and Lazy Loading:

8. Profile and Optimize:

9. Documentation:

10. Code Reviews:

Chapter 12: TypeScript and Modern Web Development

Section 12.1: Embracing Modern Web Standards with TypeScript

1. ECMAScript Modules (ESM):

2. Web APIs and DOM Manipulation:

3. Asynchronous Programming:

4. Transpilation and Polyfills:

5. Framework and Library Support:

6. ESNext Features:

Section 12.2: TypeScript in Progressive Web Apps (PWA)

1. Service Workers:

2. Web App Manifest:

3. TypeScript and Workbox:

4. PWA Auditing and Testing:

5. Building Accessible PWAs:

6. Performance Optimization:

Section 12.3: Server-Side Rendering (SSR) with TypeScript

1. Choosing an SSR Framework:

2. Creating SSR Components:

3. Server-Side Data Fetching:

4. Routing and Navigation:

5. Building and Deployment:

Section 12.4: Building Interactive Web Components with TypeScript

1. Component-Based Architecture:

2. Type-Safe Props and State:

3. Event Handling and User Interaction:

4. Reusable and Composable Components:

5. Debugging and Code Maintenance:

Section 12.5: The Future of TypeScript in Web Development

1. Deno and Beyond:

2. WebAssembly (Wasm):

3. JAMstack Architecture:

4. Serverless Computing:

5. TypeScript on the Frontend:

6. TypeScript in Progressive Web Apps (PWAs):

7. Machine Learning and AI:

8. WebAssembly Studio:

9. Community Contributions:

Chapter 13: TypeScript in Mobile App Development

Section 13.1: TypeScript with React Native

Benefits of Using TypeScript in React Native:

Integrating TypeScript in React Native:

Section 13.2: Mobile Development with Ionic and TypeScript

Benefits of Using TypeScript in Ionic:

Integrating TypeScript in Ionic:

Section 13.3: Performance Considerations for Mobile Apps

1. Lazy Loading:

2. Optimized Images:

3. Minification and Tree Shaking:

4. Caching and Offline Support:

5. Web Workers:

6. Reducing HTTP Requests:

7. Optimizing Animations:

8. Profiling and Testing:

9. Memory Management:

10. Network Optimization:

11. Battery Efficiency:

12. Cross-Platform Considerations:

Section 13.4: Cross-platform Development Strategies

1. Ionic Framework with Capacitor:

2. React Native with TypeScript:

3. Flutter with Dart:

4. Electron for Desktop Apps:

5. Web Views and Progressive Web Apps (PWAs):

6. Code Sharing Strategies:

2. Password Hashing

3. Secure Storage

4. API Security

5. Regular Security Audits

6. Compliance with Data Protection Regulations

Section 17.3: TypeScript for Secure Backend Development

1. Authentication and Authorization

2. Input Validation and Sanitization

3. Data Encryption and Storage

4. Logging and Monitoring

5. Secure Dependencies

6. Regular Security Audits

Section 17.4: Penetration Testing and Vulnerability Assessment

1. The Importance of Penetration Testing

2. Types of Penetration Testing

3. Conducting Penetration Testing

4. Vulnerability Assessment Tools

5. Regulatory Compliance

6. Continuous Testing

Chapter 1: Introduction to TypeScript

1.1 Understanding the Need for TypeScript

TypeScript has gained significant popularity in recent years as a superset of JavaScript that brings strong typing and improved tooling to the JavaScript ecosystem. In this section, we will delve into the reasons why TypeScript has become essential for modern web development and software engineering.

The Challenges of JavaScript

JavaScript, the lingua franca of the web, is known for its flexibility and ease of use. However, this flexibility can also lead to challenges, especially in large and complex codebases. JavaScript's dynamic typing allows for a wide range of programming styles, but it can also lead to runtime errors that are difficult to catch during development.

Consider a simple JavaScript function that concatenates two values:

```javascript
function concatenate(a, b) {

return a + b;

}
```

In this function, there are no type constraints, and JavaScript will happily concatenate strings or perform numeric addition depending on the input. While this flexibility can be convenient, it can also lead to unexpected behavior:

```javascript
console.log(concatenate(2, 3)); // Outputs 5

console.log(concatenate("Hello, ", "world!")); // Outputs "Hello, world!"
```

console.log(concatenate(2, "world!")); *// Outputs "2world!"*

In the third example, the function concatenates a number and a string, resulting in a less intuitive outcome.

Enter TypeScript

TypeScript addresses these challenges by introducing static typing. With TypeScript, you can declare the types of variables, function parameters, and return values, providing a clear contract for how your code should behave. Let's rewrite the concatenate function in TypeScript:

function concatenate(a: string, b: string): string {

return a + b;

}

In this TypeScript version, we explicitly declare that a and b should be of type string, and the function should return a string. If we attempt to use incompatible types, TypeScript will catch the error at compile-time:

console.log(concatenate(2, 3)); *// Error: Argument of type 'number' is not assignable to parameter of type 'string'.*

This static type checking helps catch many common programming errors before they make their way into production code.

Improved Developer Experience

Another compelling reason for using TypeScript is the enhanced developer experience. TypeScript-aware code editors provide features like autocompletion, type inference, and inline documentation, making it easier to write and maintain code.

TypeScript also allows you to leverage the latest ECMAScript features while targeting older JavaScript runtimes, ensuring your code remains compatible across browsers and platforms.

Strong Typing for Large Codebases

For large projects and teams, TypeScript's strong typing is a boon. It enables better code organization and documentation, making it easier for developers to understand and collaborate on a codebase. Additionally, TypeScript's type annotations serve as living documentation, reducing the need for extensive comments.

In summary, TypeScript offers a solution to many of the challenges faced by JavaScript developers. It provides static typing, improved tooling, and a better developer experience, making it a valuable choice for modern web development and software engineering projects. In the following sections of this chapter, we will explore the evolution of JavaScript and the rise of TypeScript, as well as the key differences between the two languages.

1.2 The Evolution of JavaScript and the Rise of TypeScript

JavaScript, initially created by Brendan Eich in just ten days, was intended as a simple scripting language for web pages. Over the years, it evolved into a versatile and ubiquitous language, powering not only web applications but also server-side development, mobile apps, and even embedded systems. However, as its usage expanded, so did the challenges associated with it. In this section, we'll explore the evolution of JavaScript and how TypeScript emerged as a solution to address some of these challenges.

The Early Days of JavaScript

JavaScript made its debut in 1995 as part of Netscape Navigator, one of the earliest web browsers. Initially named "LiveScript," it was quickly renamed "JavaScript" when Netscape entered into a partnership with Sun Microsystems. JavaScript's primary role was to enhance the interactivity of web pages by allowing developers to manipulate the Document Object Model (DOM) dynamically.

As web applications grew in complexity, JavaScript's capabilities were extended through the addition of features like XMLHttpRequest, which enabled asynchronous communication with web servers. This marked the beginning of JavaScript's journey from a simple scripting language to a full-fledged programming language for the web.

Challenges with JavaScript

While JavaScript's evolution was impressive, it also brought challenges. JavaScript's dynamic typing, a feature that allowed flexibility in the early days, became a source of concern as web applications became more substantial. Bugs stemming from type mismatches and runtime errors were common and often difficult to debug. Additionally, the lack of module systems and proper encapsulation made it challenging to manage large codebases.

Here's an example of a common JavaScript issue related to type coercion:

```
console.log(1 + "2"); // Outputs "12" instead of 3
```

In this case, JavaScript implicitly converts the number 1 to a string and performs string concatenation instead of numeric addition.

The Birth of TypeScript

TypeScript, developed by Microsoft, emerged as a response to the challenges posed by JavaScript's dynamically typed nature. It was first released in 2012, and it gained popularity quickly. TypeScript builds on JavaScript by adding optional static typing, interfaces, and a more robust tooling ecosystem.

With TypeScript, developers can catch type-related errors at compile-time, reducing the likelihood of runtime surprises. The same example with TypeScript would result in a compile-time error:

console.log(1 + "2"); *// Error: Operator '+' cannot be applied to types 'number' and 'string'.*

This early error detection significantly improves code quality and maintainability.

TypeScript's Growing Ecosystem

TypeScript's popularity has led to widespread adoption, both in open-source projects and industry giants like Google, Airbnb, and Slack. Its robust type system, coupled with excellent tooling, has made it an attractive choice for large codebases and collaborative development.

In the subsequent chapters of this book, we will explore TypeScript in-depth, covering its syntax, advanced features, migration strategies, and its application in various domains, from web and mobile development to IoT and game development. TypeScript's evolution continues, and its future looks promising as it continues to adapt to the ever-changing landscape of modern web development.

1.3 Key Differences Between JavaScript and

TypeScript

JavaScript and TypeScript share a common ancestry, but they exhibit significant differences that set them apart. In this section, we will explore these key distinctions, highlighting how TypeScript builds upon JavaScript's foundation to provide enhanced development capabilities.

1. Static Typing vs. Dynamic Typing

The most apparent difference between JavaScript and TypeScript is their approach to typing. JavaScript is dynamically typed, meaning variables can change types at runtime. While this flexibility allows for quick prototyping, it can also lead to type-related errors that are challenging to catch until runtime.

TypeScript, on the other hand, introduces static typing. You declare the types of variables, function parameters, and return values in advance. This provides early error detection during development, as the TypeScript compiler can catch type-related issues at compile-time, reducing the risk of runtime errors.

2. Optional vs. Strong Typing

JavaScript relies on optional type annotations through comments or developer conventions. For example, a comment might indicate the expected types of variables:

// @type {string}

let name = "John";

TypeScript enforces strong typing through explicit type annotations in the code. The same variable declaration in TypeScript looks like this:

```
let name: string = "John";
```

This strong typing provides better documentation and aids in code understanding, making it easier for developers to work with codebases, especially large ones.

3. Type Inference

TypeScript includes a powerful type inference system that can often infer types automatically, reducing the need for explicit type annotations. JavaScript lacks this capability, requiring developers to specify types manually.

For example, TypeScript can infer the type of a variable like this:

```
let age = 30; // TypeScript infers 'number' type
```

4. Interfaces and Type Definitions

JavaScript does not have native constructs for defining interfaces or type definitions. While documentation and conventions can be used to communicate expected data structures, there is no formal mechanism for defining and enforcing these structures.

TypeScript introduces interfaces and type definitions, allowing developers to declare the shape of objects, making it clear what properties and methods an object should have. This enhances code clarity and helps catch type-related errors early in development.

```
interface Person {

name: string;

age: number;

}
```

```typescript
function greet(person: Person) {

return `Hello, ${person.name}!`;

}
```

5. Tooling and IDE Support

TypeScript's strong typing and explicit type annotations provide an excellent foundation for tooling and integrated development environments (IDEs). Many popular code editors offer TypeScript support, providing features like autocompletion, code navigation, and refactoring assistance.

JavaScript tooling, while improving over the years, does not offer the same level of type-awareness and code analysis as TypeScript.

6. Compilation Step

JavaScript runs directly in web browsers or server environments without a compilation step. In contrast, TypeScript requires compilation to produce standard JavaScript code that can be executed. This compilation step is performed by the TypeScript compiler (tsc) before deploying code to production.

While the compilation step adds an extra build process, it ensures that TypeScript code is transformed into JavaScript that runs reliably across different environments.

7. Compatibility with Existing JavaScript

One of TypeScript's strengths is its compatibility with existing JavaScript codebases. You can gradually adopt TypeScript by renaming .js files to .ts and adding type annotations incrementally. TypeScript allows you to leverage JavaScript libraries and code seamlessly, making it a practical choice for migrating existing projects.

In summary, TypeScript builds on JavaScript's foundation by introducing static typing, strong typing, interfaces, and type inference. These key differences enhance code quality, improve developer productivity, and make TypeScript a valuable choice for modern software development.

1.4 Benefits of Migrating to TypeScript

Migrating an existing JavaScript codebase to TypeScript can be a significant undertaking, but it comes with numerous benefits that make it a compelling choice for many development teams. In this section, we'll explore the advantages of migrating to TypeScript, which range from improved code quality to enhanced developer productivity.

1. Early Error Detection

One of the most significant advantages of TypeScript is its ability to catch type-related errors at compile-time. This means that many common programming mistakes, such as passing the wrong types of arguments to functions or accessing properties that don't exist on an object, are caught before the code even runs. This early error detection leads to more robust and bug-free code.

2. Improved Code Quality

TypeScript's strong typing encourages better code quality by providing clear and self-documenting type annotations. This makes the codebase easier to understand, reduces the likelihood of runtime errors, and helps prevent unexpected behavior. Additionally, TypeScript's interfaces and type definitions make it easier to define and enforce consistent data structures and contracts throughout the codebase.

3. Enhanced Developer Experience

Developers working with TypeScript benefit from enhanced tooling and IDE support. Code editors like Visual Studio Code offer features such as autocompletion, type inference, and on-the-fly error checking, which significantly improve the developer experience. This results in faster and more efficient development workflows.

4. Code Refactoring and Navigation

TypeScript's type-awareness also provides significant advantages for code refactoring and navigation. Renaming variables, functions, or types can be done safely and efficiently with confidence that the changes will propagate correctly throughout the codebase. Developers can easily navigate through the code, jump to type definitions, and find references, simplifying maintenance and code comprehension.

5. Collaboration and Documentation

TypeScript's type annotations serve as living documentation for the codebase, making it easier for developers to collaborate. When working in a team, TypeScript provides a shared understanding of data structures and function contracts, reducing miscommunication and ensuring that everyone is on the same page. Additionally, TypeScript's self-documenting nature reduces the need for extensive code comments.

6. Seamless Integration with JavaScript

Migrating to TypeScript doesn't mean abandoning existing JavaScript code. TypeScript is fully compatible with JavaScript, allowing you to incrementally migrate code and adopt TypeScript at your own pace. You can rename .js files to .ts and add type annotations gradually, making the transition smooth and non-disruptive.

7. Third-party Library Support

TypeScript has excellent support for third-party libraries and packages. Many popular JavaScript libraries and frameworks now include TypeScript type definitions, enabling type checking and autocompletion when using these libraries in a TypeScript project. This helps maintain type safety even when integrating external code.

8. Ecosystem and Community

TypeScript has a thriving ecosystem and a large and active community. This means access to a wealth of resources, libraries, and tools that can accelerate development. TypeScript's community-driven development ensures that the language continues to evolve and adapt to the needs of modern web development.

9. Long-term Maintainability

Migrating to TypeScript is an investment in the long-term maintainability of your codebase. With TypeScript, you can write code that is less error-prone, easier to understand, and more adaptable to changing requirements. This reduces technical debt and lowers the cost of maintaining and evolving the software over time.

In conclusion, while migrating an existing JavaScript codebase to TypeScript may require some initial effort, the benefits it brings in terms of early error detection, improved code quality, enhanced developer experience, and long-term maintainability make it a compelling choice for many development projects. TypeScript's gradual adoption approach allows you to enjoy these advantages while preserving compatibility with your existing JavaScript code.

1.5 Overview of the Book Structure

In this section, we'll provide an overview of the structure of this book to help you navigate and understand its contents. "TypeScript in Practice" covers a wide range of topics related to TypeScript, from its basics to advanced application scenarios. Here's a breakdown of what you can expect in each chapter:

Chapter 1: Introduction to TypeScript

This chapter, where you are currently, introduces you to TypeScript and its significance in modern web development. It covers the need for TypeScript, its evolution from JavaScript, key differences, benefits, and a glimpse of what you'll find in the subsequent chapters.

Chapter 2: TypeScript Basics

Chapter 2 delves into the fundamentals of TypeScript. You'll learn about TypeScript's syntax, setting up a TypeScript environment, basic types, functions, methods, interfaces, and classes. This chapter provides the essential building blocks for writing TypeScript code.

Chapter 3: Advanced TypeScript Features

Building upon the basics, Chapter 3 explores advanced features of TypeScript. Topics include generics, decorators, namespaces, modules, compiler options, and advanced type manipulation techniques. You'll gain a deeper understanding of TypeScript's capabilities.

Chapter 4: Migrating from JavaScript to TypeScript

Chapter 4 is dedicated to helping you migrate your existing JavaScript code to TypeScript. It covers the preparation, step-by-step migration process, common challenges, leveraging TypeScript in existing projects, and best practices for post-migration.

Chapter 5: Type Safety and Error Handling

This chapter focuses on the importance of type safety and effective error handling in TypeScript. It discusses strategies for error handling, utilizing TypeScript for debugging, creating custom types for error handling, and provides practical examples.

Chapter 6: Working with Libraries and Frameworks

Chapter 6 explores integrating TypeScript with popular JavaScript libraries and frameworks. Topics include TypeScript in React, Angular, Vue, managing types in third-party libraries, building custom libraries, and best practices for framework integration.

Chapter 7: TypeScript in Backend Development

Chapter 7 covers TypeScript's role in backend development. It explains setting up a TypeScript Node.js project, working with Express.js and other backend frameworks, managing database interactions, building RESTful APIs, and addressing performance considerations.

Chapter 8: Testing and Quality Assurance

In this chapter, you'll learn about testing TypeScript code. It covers writing unit tests, integration testing strategies, end-to-end testing, code quality tools, and continuous integration and deployment with TypeScript.

Chapter 9: Advanced TypeScript Patterns

Chapter 9 dives into advanced patterns in TypeScript. Topics include design patterns, functional programming techniques, reactive programming, TypeScript decorators in depth, and advanced asynchronous patterns.

Chapter 10: TypeScript for Scalable Projects

Chapter 10 focuses on using TypeScript in large-scale projects. It discusses organizing codebases, scalability best practices, modularization, TypeScript in microservices architecture, and managing dependencies in large projects.

Chapter 11: Performance Optimization in TypeScript

This chapter is dedicated to optimizing TypeScript code for performance. It covers understanding performance overheads, profiling and benchmarking, code optimization techniques, memory management, and tips for efficient coding.

Chapter 12: TypeScript and Modern Web Development

Chapter 12 explores TypeScript's role in modern web development. Topics include embracing modern web standards, TypeScript in Progressive Web Apps (PWA), server-side rendering (SSR), building interactive web components, and the future of TypeScript in web development.

Chapter 13: TypeScript in Mobile App Development

In this chapter, you'll discover how TypeScript can be used in mobile app development. Topics include TypeScript with React Native, mobile development with Ionic and TypeScript, performance considerations, cross-platform strategies, and case studies of successful TypeScript mobile apps.

Chapter 14: DevOps and TypeScript

Chapter 14 delves into TypeScript's role in DevOps practices. It covers automating builds and deployments with TypeScript, TypeScript in containerized environments, monitoring and logging TypeScript applications, and TypeScript in microservice orchestration.

Chapter 15: TypeScript and the Cloud

This chapter explores TypeScript in cloud-native development. Topics include TypeScript with cloud providers like AWS, Azure, and Google Cloud, serverless architectures, building and deploying cloud functions, and managing cloud resources with TypeScript.

Chapter 16: TypeScript for Game Development

Chapter 16 discusses using TypeScript in game development. It covers setting up a game development environment, TypeScript in Canvas and WebGL, integrating physics and animation libraries, TypeScript in multiplayer game development, and case studies of TypeScript in popular games.

Chapter 17: Security Practices in TypeScript

This chapter focuses on security best practices in TypeScript development. Topics include handling sensitive data, secure backend development, penetration testing, vulnerability assessment, and security libraries and tools for TypeScript.

Chapter 18: Internationalization and Localization

Chapter 18 explores implementing internationalization and localization in TypeScript. Topics include handling multiple languages and cultures, date, time, and currency handling, accessibility considerations, and case studies of global apps with TypeScript.

Chapter 19: TypeScript and IoT Development

In this chapter, you'll learn about TypeScript's role in Internet of Things (IoT) development. Topics include building IoT applications with TypeScript, interfacing with hardware, networking, and communication in IoT, and real-world TypeScript IoT project examples.

Chapter 20: The Future of TypeScript

The final chapter, Chapter 20, discusses TypeScript's place in the future of development. It explores emerging trends and technologies, the evolving TypeScript ecosystem, preparing for future updates, and concludes with reflections on the ongoing journey from JavaScript to TypeScript.

Each chapter provides comprehensive coverage of its respective topic, making this book a valuable resource for developers looking to harness the power of TypeScript in various domains and scenarios.

Chapter 2: TypeScript Basics

2.1 Understanding TypeScript Syntax

TypeScript, as a superset of JavaScript, inherits much of its syntax from JavaScript. However, it also introduces some additional syntax elements and features. In this section, we will explore the fundamental aspects of TypeScript syntax, including variable declarations, data types, and basic control flow constructs.

Variable Declarations

In TypeScript, you can declare variables using the let, const, or var keywords, just like in JavaScript. However, TypeScript introduces the concept of static typing, allowing you to specify the type of a variable explicitly. Here's an example:

let message: string = "Hello, TypeScript!";

In this example, we declare a variable named message and specify that it should hold a string. TypeScript will enforce that only string values can be assigned to this variable.

Data Types

TypeScript provides various data types to represent different kinds of values. Some of the basic data types include:

- number: Represents numeric values, including integers and floating-point numbers.

- string: Represents text or character sequences.

- boolean: Represents true or false values.

- null and undefined: Special types representing the absence of a value.

- object: Represents a general object type.

- array: Represents an array of values, and you can specify the type of its elements.

let age: number = 30;

let name: string = "John";

let isStudent: boolean = **true**;

let person: object = { firstName: "Alice", lastName: "Smith" };

let numbers: number[] = [1, 2, 3, 4, 5];

Type Inference

TypeScript can often infer the type of a variable without explicit annotations, thanks to a feature called type inference. For example:

let greeting = "Hello, TypeScript!"; *// TypeScript infers 'string' type*

let count = 42; *// TypeScript infers 'number' type*

Type inference helps reduce the need for explicit type annotations while still providing type safety.

Type Annotations

While TypeScript can often infer types, you can provide explicit type annotations to clarify the expected types or to handle situations where inference might not work as intended. Here's an example:

let username: string; *// Explicit type annotation*

```
username = "john_doe";
```

Basic Control Flow

TypeScript supports standard control flow constructs like if, for, and while. Here's an example of an if statement:

```
let score = 85;

if (score >= 90) {

console.log("Excellent!");

} else if (score >= 70) {

console.log("Good job!");

} else {

console.log("Keep working on it.");

}
```

Loops work similarly to JavaScript, with for and while loops available for iteration.

Functions

Functions in TypeScript allow you to specify the types of parameters and return values. Here's a simple function declaration:

```
function add(a: number, b: number): number {

return a + b;

}
```

In this example, the function add takes two parameters of type number and returns a value of type number.

Arrow Functions

TypeScript supports arrow functions, which provide a more concise way to define functions. Here's an example:

const multiply = (x: number, y: number): number => x * y;

Arrow functions are especially useful for writing shorter, more readable code.

These are some of the fundamental aspects of TypeScript syntax. In the following sections, we'll explore TypeScript's type system in more detail, covering advanced types, interfaces, and classes. Understanding TypeScript's syntax is the foundation for effectively using the language to build robust and maintainable software.

2.2 Setting Up a TypeScript Environment

Before you can start writing TypeScript code, you need to set up a development environment that supports TypeScript. This section will guide you through the process of setting up a TypeScript environment, including installing TypeScript, configuring a TypeScript project, and integrating TypeScript with popular code editors.

Installing TypeScript

To begin, you'll need to install TypeScript globally on your system. You can do this using Node Package Manager (npm) by running the following command:

npm install -g typescript

Once TypeScript is installed, you can check the version to ensure it was installed successfully:

tsc -v

This command should display the installed TypeScript version.

Initializing a TypeScript Project

To start a new TypeScript project, you can create a new directory for your project and navigate to it in your terminal. Then, run the following command to initialize a TypeScript project:

tsc—init

This command generates a tsconfig.json file in your project directory. This file contains configuration options for TypeScript.

Configuring tsconfig.json

You can customize the tsconfig.json file to match your project's requirements. Some common configurations include specifying the target JavaScript version, enabling strict type checking, and defining the output directory for compiled JavaScript files. Here's an example of a tsconfig.json file:

{

"compilerOptions": {

"target": "ES6",

"strict": **true**,

"outDir": "./dist"

},

```
"include": ["src/**/*.ts"],

"exclude": ["node_modules"]

}
```

In this example, we target ES6 JavaScript, enable strict type checking, and specify that compiled JavaScript files should be placed in a dist directory. We also include TypeScript files under the src directory and exclude the node_modules directory from compilation.

Writing TypeScript Code

With your TypeScript environment set up and configured, you can start writing TypeScript code in .ts files. Here's a simple example:

```
// hello.ts

function sayHello(name: string) {

console.log(`Hello, ${name}!`);

}

sayHello("John");
```

Compiling TypeScript

To compile your TypeScript code into JavaScript, use the TypeScript compiler (tsc). Run the following command in your project directory:

```
tsc
```

This command will compile all TypeScript files in your project based on the tsconfig.json configuration.

Integrating with Code Editors

Popular code editors like Visual Studio Code provide excellent TypeScript support out of the box. You can open your project in Visual Studio Code, and it will automatically detect your TypeScript configuration, providing features like code completion, type checking, and inline documentation.

Running Compiled JavaScript

After compiling your TypeScript code, you can run the resulting JavaScript files using Node.js or in a web browser. For Node.js, simply use the node command:

node dist/hello.js

For web applications, you can include the compiled JavaScript files in your HTML and load them in a browser.

Setting up a TypeScript environment is the first step toward leveraging TypeScript's benefits for your projects. It allows you to write type-safe code, catch errors early, and take advantage of TypeScript's advanced tooling and editor support.

2.3 Basic Types in TypeScript

TypeScript provides a variety of basic data types that allow you to specify the type of values a variable can hold. These types help catch type-related errors at compile-time, making your code more robust and self-documenting. In this section, we'll explore some of the essential basic types in TypeScript.

Number

The number type represents numeric values, including both integers and floating-point numbers. You can declare variables with the number type like this:

let age: number = 30;

let pi: number = 3.14159;

String

The string type represents textual data. You can declare variables with the string type like this:

let name: string = "John Doe";

let message: string = 'Hello, TypeScript!';

Boolean

The boolean type represents Boolean values, which can be either true or false. You can declare variables with the boolean type like this:

let isStudent: boolean = **true**;

let hasAccount: boolean = **false**;

Array

The array type represents a collection of values of the same type. You can declare arrays in TypeScript using square brackets, followed by the type of elements in the array:

let numbers: number[] = [1, 2, 3, 4, 5];

```
let fruits: string[] = ["apple", "banana", "cherry"];
```

You can also use the generic Array type to specify the type of elements within the array:

```
let colors: Array<string> = ["red", "green", "blue"];
```

Tuple

A tuple is a fixed-size array where each element can have a different type. You define a tuple by specifying the types of its elements in a specific order:

```
let person: [string, number] = ["John Doe", 30];
```

In this example, person is a tuple with the first element as a string (name) and the second element as a number (age).

Null and Undefined

The null and undefined types represent the absence of a value. You can declare variables with these types like this:

```
let noValue: null = null;
```

```
let notDefined: undefined = undefined;
```

Any

The any type is a special type that allows a variable to hold values of any type. While it provides flexibility, it bypasses TypeScript's type checking:

```
let dynamicValue: any = 42;

dynamicValue = "Hello, TypeScript!";
```

The use of any should be minimized in favor of more specific types whenever possible to maintain type safety.

Void

The void type is used to indicate that a function does not return any value:

```typescript
function logMessage(message: string): void {

console.log(message);

}
```

Enum

An enum is a way to define a set of named constants, often representing a set of related values:

```typescript
enum Color {

Red,

Green,

Blue,

}

let selectedColor: Color = Color.Red;
```

In this example, Color is an enum with three values: Red, Green, and Blue. selectedColor can only hold one of these enum values.

These are some of the basic types in TypeScript. Understanding and using these types effectively is essential for writing type-safe and maintainable code. In the next sections, we'll explore more advanced types and how to work with them in TypeScript.

2.4 Functions and Methods in TypeScript

Functions play a fundamental role in any programming language, and TypeScript is no exception. TypeScript allows you to define functions with strong typing, enabling you to specify the types of function parameters and return values. In this section, we'll explore how to work with functions and methods in TypeScript.

Function Declarations

In TypeScript, you can declare functions using the function keyword. You can specify the types of function parameters and the return type. Here's an example of a function that takes two numbers and returns their sum:

```typescript
function addNumbers(a: number, b: number): number {

return a + b;

}
```

In this example, addNumbers is a function that takes two parameters, a and b, both of type number, and returns a value of type number.

Function Expressions

You can also define functions using function expressions, which are often assigned to variables. Function expressions allow you to specify the function's type directly in the assignment. Here's an example:

```typescript
const subtractNumbers = function (a: number, b: number): number {

return a - b;
```

```
};
```

In this example, subtractNumbers is a variable containing a function expression. TypeScript infers the function's type based on the assignment, but you can also explicitly specify the type if needed.

Arrow Functions

Arrow functions provide a concise way to define functions, especially when the function is simple and consists of a single expression. Here's an example:

```typescript
const multiply = (x: number, y: number): number => x * y;
```

In this example, multiply is an arrow function that takes two parameters, x and y, both of type number, and returns their product. Arrow functions automatically capture the surrounding context, making them suitable for callback functions and event handlers.

Optional Parameters

You can make function parameters optional by adding a question mark ? after their names in the parameter list. This allows you to call the function without providing values for those parameters. Here's an example:

```typescript
function greet(name: string, age?: number): string {

if (age === undefined) {

return `Hello, ${name}!`;

} else {

return `Hello, ${name}, you are ${age} years old!`;

}
```

```
}
```

In this example, the age parameter is optional. If you provide an age when calling greet, it includes the age in the greeting; otherwise, it omits it.

Default Parameters

You can also specify default values for parameters in TypeScript functions. If a parameter is not provided when calling the function, it takes the default value. Here's an example:

```typescript
function greetWithDefault(name: string, greeting = "Hello"): string {

return `${greeting}, ${name}!`;

}
```

In this example, if you call greetWithDefault("Alice"), it defaults to "Hello, Alice!". However, you can still override the default value by providing a different greeting.

Rest Parameters

Rest parameters allow you to represent an indefinite number of arguments as an array. You can use the rest parameter syntax (...) before the parameter name to indicate that it will collect the remaining arguments into an array. Here's an example:

```typescript
function sumAll(...numbers: number[]): number {

return numbers.reduce((total, num) => total + num, 0);

}
```

In this example, sumAll accepts any number of arguments and calculates their sum using the reduce method.

Function Overloading

TypeScript supports function overloading, which allows you to define multiple function signatures for the same function name based on the number or types of arguments. TypeScript will then choose the appropriate signature based on the function call. Here's an example:

```typescript
function combine(a: string, b: string): string;

function combine(a: number, b: number): number;

function combine(a: any, b: any): any {

return a + b;

}
```

In this example, the combine function is overloaded to accept both strings and numbers. Depending on the arguments you provide, TypeScript selects the correct signature and enforces type safety.

Method Declarations

In TypeScript, you can declare methods inside classes. Methods are similar to functions but are associated with an object instance. Here's an example of a class with a method:

```typescript
class Calculator {

add(a: number, b: number): number {

return a + b;
```

```
}

}
```

In this example, the Calculator class has an add method that takes two numbers and returns their sum. You can create instances of the Calculator class and call the add method on them.

Understanding how to define and use functions and methods in TypeScript is crucial for building structured and type-safe applications. Functions provide a way to encapsulate behavior and promote reusability in your code.

2.5 Interfaces and Classes in TypeScript

Interfaces and classes are fundamental constructs in object-oriented programming, and TypeScript provides strong support for them. In this section, we'll explore how to define and use interfaces and classes in TypeScript to create structured and type-safe code.

Interfaces

An interface in TypeScript defines a contract that a class or object must adhere to. It specifies the structure and types of properties and methods that the implementing class or object should have. Here's an example of defining an interface:

```
interface Person {

firstName: string;

lastName: string;

age: number;

}
```

```typescript
const person: Person = {

firstName: "John",

lastName: "Doe",

age: 30,

};
```

In this example, we define an interface Person with properties firstName, lastName, and age. Then, we create an object person that conforms to this interface.

Interfaces can also define methods:

```typescript
interface Shape {

area(): number;

}

class Circle implements Shape {

constructor(private radius: number) {}

area(): number {

return Math.PI * this.radius * this.radius;

}

}

const circle = new Circle(5);

console.log(`Circle area: ${circle.area()}`);
```

Here, we define an interface Shape with a method area(). The Circle class implements this interface, providing an implementation for the area method.

Interfaces are powerful tools for ensuring that objects adhere to a specific structure and contract, making code more predictable and maintainable.

Classes

Classes in TypeScript are blueprints for creating objects with properties and methods. They provide a way to encapsulate data and behavior into a single unit. Here's an example of defining a class:

```typescript
class Animal {

constructor(public name: string, public species: string) {}

makeSound(sound: string): void {

console.log(`${this.name} the ${this.species} makes a ${sound} sound.`);

}

}

const lion = new Animal("Leo", "Lion");

lion.makeSound("roaring");
```

In this example, we create a Animal class with a constructor that sets name and species properties. The class also has a makeSound method.

You can extend classes in TypeScript to create subclasses and inherit properties and methods:

```
class Bird extends Animal {

fly(): void {

console.log(`${this.name} the ${this.species} is flying.`);

}

}

const eagle = new Bird("Eddie", "Eagle");

eagle.fly();
```

Here, we extend the Animal class to create a Bird subclass with an additional fly method.

Access Modifiers

TypeScript provides access modifiers like public, private, and protected to control the visibility of class members (properties and methods). For example:

```
class Car {

private speed: number;

constructor(speed: number) {

this.speed = speed;

}

accelerate(): void {

this.speed += 10;

}
```

}

In this example, the speed property is marked as private, meaning it can only be accessed within the class.

Abstract Classes

Abstract classes are classes that cannot be instantiated directly but serve as a base for other classes. They can have abstract methods that must be implemented by derived classes. Here's an example:

abstract class Shape {

abstract area(): number;

}

class Circle **extends** Shape {

constructor(**private** radius: number) {

super();

}

area(): number {

return Math.PI * **this**.radius * **this**.radius;

}

}

In this example, Shape is an abstract class with an abstract area method. The Circle class extends Shape and provides an implementation for the area method.

Interfaces and classes are essential for creating structured and reusable code in TypeScript. They help define contracts, encapsulate behavior, and promote code organization and maintainability. Understanding how to use them effectively is key to building robust TypeScript applications.

Chapter 3: Advanced TypeScript Features

3.1 Generics and Advanced Types

Generics are a powerful feature in TypeScript that allow you to create reusable and type-safe components, functions, and classes. They enable you to write code that works with different data types while maintaining type safety. In this section, we'll explore generics and some advanced type features in TypeScript.

Understanding Generics

Generics are placeholders for types that you can use when defining functions, classes, or interfaces. They allow you to write code that is more flexible and can work with various data types. Generics are denoted by angle brackets <T>, where T can be replaced with any type name.

Using Generics in Functions

Let's start with a simple example of a generic function that swaps the values of two variables:

```
function swap<T>(a: T, b: T): void {

let temp: T = a;

a = b;

b = temp;

}
```

```typescript
let a = 5;

let b = 10;

swap(a, b);

console.log(`a: ${a}, b: ${b}`); // Output: a: 10, b: 5
```

In this example, we define a swap function that takes two generic parameters a and b. The function swaps the values of a and b, and we can use it with different data types while maintaining type safety.

Using Generics in Classes

You can also use generics when defining classes. Here's an example of a generic Stack class:

```typescript
class Stack<T> {

private items: T[] = [];

push(item: T): void {

this.items.push(item);

}

pop(): T | undefined {

return this.items.pop();

}

peek(): T | undefined {

return this.items[this.items.length - 1];

}
```

```typescript
isEmpty(): boolean {

return this.items.length === 0;

}

}

const numberStack = new Stack<number>();

numberStack.push(1);

numberStack.push(2);

numberStack.push(3);

const stringStack = new Stack<string>();

stringStack.push("apple");

stringStack.push("banana");

stringStack.push("cherry");
```

In this example, the Stack class uses a generic type T to define the type of items it can hold. We can create Stack instances for different data types, such as number and string.

Advanced Types

TypeScript provides advanced type features that allow you to manipulate and transform types in various ways. Some of these advanced types include:

Union Types

Union types allow you to specify that a value can have one of several possible types. For example:

```typescript
let username: string | null = getUser() || null;
```

Here, username can be a string or null.

Intersection Types

Intersection types allow you to combine multiple types into a single type. For example:

```typescript
type Person = { name: string };

type Employee = { employeeId: number };

type EmployeePerson = Person & Employee;

const employee: EmployeePerson = {

name: "John",

employeeId: 12345,

};
```

In this example, EmployeePerson is a type that combines properties from both Person and Employee types.

Conditional Types

Conditional types allow you to create types that depend on conditions. They are often used in generic types. For example:

```typescript
type IsString<T> = T extends string ? true : false;

const isString: IsString<string> = true; // true

const isNotString: IsString<number> = false; // false
```

In this example, IsString is a conditional type that checks if T extends string and returns true or false accordingly.

Mapped Types

Mapped types allow you to create new types by transforming the properties of an existing type. For example:

```typescript
type Person = { name: string; age: number };

type ReadOnly<T> = {

readonly [K in keyof T]: T[K];

};

const readOnlyPerson: ReadOnly<Person> = {

name: "Alice",

age: 30,

};

readOnlyPerson.name = "Bob"; // Error: Cannot assign to 'name' because it is a read-only property.
```

In this example, the ReadOnly mapped type creates a new type with all properties of Person made read-only.

Generics and advanced types are powerful tools that allow you to write flexible and type-safe code in TypeScript. They enable you to create reusable components and work with different data types while benefiting from TypeScript's strong type checking. Understanding and mastering these features can significantly improve your TypeScript programming skills.

3.2 Decorators and Mixins

Decorators and mixins are advanced features in TypeScript that enable you to add functionality and behavior to classes and objects in a modular and reusable way. In this section, we'll explore decorators and mixins and how they can be used in TypeScript.

Decorators

Decorators are a way to add metadata and behavior to classes, methods, properties, or parameters in TypeScript. They are commonly used in frameworks like Angular and NestJS for various purposes, such as defining routes, authentication, and validation.

To create a decorator, you define a function that takes specific parameters and applies the decorator using the @ symbol. Here's a simple example of a class decorator:

```typescript
function myClassDecorator(target: Function) {

// Add behavior to the class constructor

target.prototype.sayHello = function () {

console.log("Hello from decorated class!");

};

}

@myClassDecorator
```

```typescript
class DecoratedClass {}

const instance = new DecoratedClass();

instance.sayHello(); // Output: Hello from decorated class!
```

In this example, the myClassDecorator function is a class decorator that adds a sayHello method to the decorated class. When you create an instance of DecoratedClass, it can call the sayHello method.

You can also create decorators for methods, properties, and parameters, allowing you to enhance or modify their behavior.

Mixins

Mixins are a way to combine the functionality of multiple classes into a single class. They provide a mechanism for code reuse and composition in a more flexible way than traditional inheritance.

Here's an example of creating a mixin for logging:

```typescript
class LoggerMixin {

log(message: string) {

console.log(`[Log]: ${message}`);

}

}

class MyClass implements LoggerMixin {

constructor(private name: string) {}

logName() {

this.log(`Name: ${this.name}`);
```

```
}

}
```

```typescript
const myInstance = new MyClass("John");

myInstance.logName(); // Output: [Log]: Name: John
```

In this example, the LoggerMixin class provides a log method for logging. The MyClass class implements LoggerMixin, allowing it to use the log method.

Mixins can be composed in various ways, allowing you to create classes with multiple behaviors from different mixins.

Combining Decorators and Mixins

You can combine decorators and mixins to create powerful and modular code in TypeScript. For example, you can create decorators that apply mixins to classes:

```typescript
function withLogger(target: Function) {

return class extends target {

logger = new LoggerMixin();

log(message: string) {

this.logger.log(message);

}

};

}

@withLogger
```

```typescript
class LoggableClass {

constructor(private name: string) {}

logName() {

this.log(`Name: ${this.name}`);

}

}

const loggableInstance = new LoggableClass("Alice");

loggableInstance.logName(); // Output: [Log]: Name: Alice
```

In this example, the withLogger decorator adds logging functionality to the LoggableClass by applying the LoggerMixin.

Decorators and mixins are advanced TypeScript features that can greatly enhance code modularity, reusability, and maintainability. They allow you to add and compose behaviors in a flexible and organized manner, making your code more powerful and easier to work with. Understanding and using these features effectively can be particularly beneficial in larger and more complex TypeScript projects.

3.3 Working with Namespaces and Modules

In TypeScript, namespaces and modules are used to organize and structure code into smaller, manageable units. They help prevent naming conflicts and allow for better code separation and encapsulation. In this section, we'll explore namespaces and modules in TypeScript and how they can be used effectively.

Namespaces

Namespaces provide a way to encapsulate code and prevent naming collisions in a global scope. They are a way to group related code together and expose it as a single entity. To define a namespace, you use the namespace keyword:

```
namespace MyNamespace {

export function sayHello() {

console.log("Hello from MyNamespace!");

}

}

MyNamespace.sayHello(); // Output: Hello from MyNamespace!
```

In this example, we define a namespace MyNamespace that contains a sayHello function. The export keyword is used to make the function accessible outside the namespace.

Namespaces can also be nested, allowing for further organization of code:

```
namespace OuterNamespace {

export namespace InnerNamespace {

export function greet() {

console.log("Greetings from InnerNamespace!");

}

}
```

```
}
```

OuterNamespace.InnerNamespace.greet(); *// Output: Greetings from InnerNamespace!*

Using namespaces helps avoid global scope pollution and makes it easier to manage large codebases by organizing related code into logical units.

Modules

Modules are a more modern and widely adopted way to structure and organize code in TypeScript. They are similar to namespaces but offer better support for handling dependencies and encapsulation.

To create a module, you can use the export keyword to expose variables, functions, classes, or other constructs that can be imported by other parts of your code. Here's an example of creating and using a module:

// MathOperations.ts

export function add(a: number, b: number): number {

return a + b;

```
}
```

// main.ts

import { add } **from** "./MathOperations";

console.log(add(5, 3)); *// Output: 8*

In this example, we have a module MathOperations in a separate file. We export the add function, and in the main.ts file, we import and use it.

Modules can be organized into a hierarchical structure, and TypeScript provides various module systems like CommonJS, AMD, and ES6 (ES2015) for different use cases.

Namespace vs. Module

While both namespaces and modules can be used for organizing code, modules are generally preferred in modern TypeScript development due to their better support for dependency management, bundling, and compatibility with various module systems.

Namespaces are still useful in certain scenarios, especially when working with legacy code or third-party libraries that use namespaces.

Using Triple-Slash Directives

To reference external declaration files or declare modules in TypeScript, you can use triple-slash directives at the top of your file. For example:

```
/// <reference path="my-library.d.ts" />
```

```
import { MyModule } from "my-library";
```

Triple-slash directives provide information to the TypeScript compiler about dependencies and declarations.

Declaration Files

When working with external libraries or JavaScript code, you may need to create declaration files (with a .d.ts extension) to provide type information for the code. Declaration files allow TypeScript to understand the types used in JavaScript code.

In summary, namespaces and modules are essential tools for organizing and structuring code in TypeScript projects. Modules are typically preferred for modern projects, while namespaces can still be useful in specific cases. Understanding how to use namespaces and modules effectively can significantly improve code maintainability and organization.

3.4 TypeScript Compiler Options

The TypeScript compiler (tsc) provides a wide range of options and configurations to tailor the compilation process to your specific needs. These options allow you to control how TypeScript handles type checking, module resolution, output format, and more. In this section, we'll explore some of the most commonly used TypeScript compiler options.

Basic Compilation

To compile a TypeScript file, you can use the tsc command followed by the filename. For example:

tsc myFile.ts

This command compiles myFile.ts into JavaScript, generating an output file named myFile.js by default.

Output Configuration

You can control the output format and location using compiler options. Here are some commonly used output-related options:

- —outDir: Specifies the directory where compiled output files should be placed. For example, tsc—outDir dist compiles files into the dist directory.

- —outFile: Combines multiple output files into a single file. For example, tsc—outFile bundle.js generates a single JavaScript file named bundle.js from multiple TypeScript files.

Module Resolution

TypeScript supports different module systems, including CommonJS, AMD, ES6, and more. You can specify the module system you want to target using the —module option:

- —module commonjs: Generates CommonJS modules.

- —module amd: Generates AMD modules.

- —module es6: Generates ES6 modules.

- —module system: Generates SystemJS modules.

Target JavaScript Version

You can specify the ECMAScript target version using the —target option. For example:

- —target es5: Compiles TypeScript to ES5 JavaScript.

- —target es6: Compiles TypeScript to ES6 JavaScript.

- —target esnext: Compiles TypeScript to the latest ECMAScript version supported by your environment.

Type Checking

TypeScript provides strong type checking by default, but you can configure the strictness of type checking using various options:

- —strict: Enables strict type checking options such as noImplicitAny, strictNullChecks, and strictFunctionTypes.

- —noImplicitAny: Flags variables with an implicit any type as an error.

- —strictNullChecks: Checks for null and undefined values more rigorously.

Source Map Generation

Source maps allow you to debug your TypeScript code in the original TypeScript files instead of the compiled JavaScript. You can enable source map generation with the —sourceMap option:

tsc—sourceMap myFile.ts

This generates a .js.map file alongside the compiled JavaScript file.

Watch Mode

To automatically recompile TypeScript files when they change, you can use the —watch option:

tsc—watch myFile.ts

This keeps the compiler running in watch mode, monitoring for changes and recompiling as needed.

Configuration Files

You can create a tsconfig.json file to store all your compiler options in a single configuration file. This file allows you to specify compiler options and include or exclude files or directories from compilation. Here's a minimal tsconfig.json example:

```
{

"compilerOptions": {

"outDir": "./dist",

"target": "es5"

},

"include": ["src/**/*.ts"],

"exclude": ["node_modules"]

}
```

With a tsconfig.json file in place, you can simply run tsc without any arguments to compile your TypeScript code based on the configuration defined in the file.

These are some of the most commonly used TypeScript compiler options. Understanding and configuring these options according to your project's needs can help you fine-tune the compilation process and improve your development workflow.

3.5 Advanced Type Manipulation Techniques

TypeScript provides advanced type manipulation features that allow you to create complex and precise types to handle various scenarios. In this section, we'll explore some of these techniques, including conditional types, mapped types, type inference, and type casting.

Conditional Types

Conditional types allow you to create types that depend on conditions. They are often used in generic types to make decisions based on the types of input. Here's an example of a conditional type:

```typescript
type IsString<T> = T extends string ? true : false;

const isString: IsString<string> = true; // true

const isNotString: IsString<number> = false; // false
```

In this example, the IsString conditional type checks if the provided type T extends string and returns true or false accordingly. Conditional types are powerful for creating flexible type definitions.

Mapped Types

Mapped types allow you to create new types by transforming the properties of an existing type. Here's an example:

```typescript
type Person = { name: string; age: number };

type ReadOnly<T> = {

readonly [K in keyof T]: T[K];

};

const readOnlyPerson: ReadOnly<Person> = {

name: "Alice",

age: 30,

};
```

readOnlyPerson.name = "Bob"; *// Error: Cannot assign to 'name' because it is a read-only property.*

In this example, the ReadOnly mapped type creates a new type where all properties of Person are made read-only. Mapped types are useful for enforcing immutability and creating variations of existing types.

Type Inference

Type inference allows TypeScript to automatically determine the type of a variable based on its value. For example:

const message = "Hello, TypeScript!";

// TypeScript infers the type of 'message' as 'string'

const numbers = [1, 2, 3];

// TypeScript infers the type of 'numbers' as 'number[]'

Type inference helps catch type-related errors early in development and reduces the need for explicit type annotations.

Type Casting

Type casting is a way to assert or convert the type of a variable. TypeScript provides two syntaxes for type casting: angle brackets and the as keyword. Here's an example using the as keyword:

const value: any = "Hello, TypeScript!";

const length = (value **as** string).length;

In this example, we use the as keyword to cast value to a string type to access the length property. Type casting should be used with caution, as it bypasses type checking.

Template Literal Types

Template literal types allow you to create string literal types that are based on template strings. For example:

```typescript
type Greeting = `Hello, ${string}!`;

const greeting: Greeting = "Hello, TypeScript!";
```

Template literal types are particularly useful when working with string manipulation and ensuring type safety.

Intersection and Union Types

Intersection types (&) allow you to combine multiple types into a single type with all the properties of each type. Union types (|) allow a value to have one of several possible types. For example:

```typescript
type Person = { name: string };

type Employee = { employeeId: number };

type EmployeePerson = Person & Employee;

const employee: EmployeePerson = {

name: "John",

employeeId: 12345,

};
```

In this example, EmployeePerson is an intersection type that combines properties from both Person and Employee types.

These advanced type manipulation techniques in TypeScript provide the flexibility and precision needed to create complex and robust type definitions for your applications. Mastering these techniques allows you to harness the full power of TypeScript's static type checking and code analysis capabilities.

Chapter 4: Migrating from JavaScript to TypeScript

4.1 Preparing Your JavaScript Code for Migration

Migrating from JavaScript to TypeScript is a process that involves adding static typing to your existing codebase. TypeScript provides a smooth migration path, allowing you to gradually introduce types while still working with your JavaScript code. In this section, we'll discuss the preparation steps and best practices for migrating your JavaScript code to TypeScript.

Assessing Your Project

Before you begin the migration process, it's essential to assess your project's size, complexity, and goals. Consider the following questions:

- How large is your codebase?

- What are your project's long-term maintenance needs?

- Are there specific areas where type safety is critical?

- Do you have a clear understanding of TypeScript and its benefits?

Based on your assessment, you can decide on the migration approach that best suits your project.

Setting Up a TypeScript Environment

To start the migration, you need to set up a TypeScript environment within your project. Follow these steps:

1. **Install TypeScript**: Use npm or yarn to install TypeScript as a development dependency:

npm install typescript—save-dev

1. **Create a tsconfig.json file**: Use the tsc—init command to generate a tsconfig.json configuration file. This file allows you to specify TypeScript compiler options and includes/excludes files for compilation.
2. **Install Type Definitions (if needed)**: If your project uses external libraries, you may need to install type definitions for those libraries. Many libraries have type definitions available on DefinitelyTyped.

Start with Strict Flags

TypeScript provides several "strict" flags that enable a higher level of type checking. It's a good practice to enable these flags gradually during the migration process. Some important strict flags include:

- —strict: Enforces strict type checking options, including noImplicitAny, strictNullChecks, and strictFunctionTypes.

- —noImplicitAny: Flags variables with an implicit any type as an error. This is a useful flag to enable early in the migration process.

- —strictNullChecks: Ensures that variables are not used before they are assigned a value and checks for null and undefined values more rigorously.

Annotate Types

Start annotating types for variables, function parameters, and return values in your JavaScript code. TypeScript uses type annotations to provide static type checking. Here's an example of adding type annotations:

```
// JavaScript

function add(a, b) {

return a + b;

}

// TypeScript

function add(a: number, b: number): number {

return a + b;

}
```

By gradually adding type annotations, you improve the type safety of your code while retaining compatibility with existing JavaScript.

Use JSDoc Type Annotations

If you prefer not to use TypeScript's native type annotations, you can use JSDoc comments to annotate types in your JavaScript code. TypeScript will recognize JSDoc annotations and provide type checking based on them. Here's an example:

```
/**

* @param {number} a

* @param {number} b

* @returns {number}

*/

function add(a, b) {

return a + b;

}
```

Address Type Incompatibilities

During the migration, you may encounter type incompatibilities between your JavaScript code and TypeScript. These issues can often be resolved by adjusting your code or introducing explicit type annotations. Pay attention to cases where TypeScript cannot infer types accurately and provide explicit type information.

Testing and Validation

Throughout the migration process, it's crucial to thoroughly test and validate your code. Write unit tests to ensure that your code behaves as expected with TypeScript's type checking. This helps catch potential issues early and ensures the correctness of your codebase.

In summary, preparing your JavaScript code for migration to TypeScript involves assessing your project, setting up a TypeScript environment, enabling strict type checking, annotating types, and addressing any type incompatibilities. Gradually introducing TypeScript into your codebase allows you to enjoy the benefits of static typing while maintaining compatibility with your existing JavaScript code.

4.2 Step-by-Step Migration Process

Migrating from JavaScript to TypeScript is a gradual process that involves converting your codebase incrementally. This section outlines a step-by-step migration process to help you transition smoothly.

1. Start with a TypeScript File

Begin by creating a new TypeScript file within your project. You can choose a specific module, component, or feature to start with. This TypeScript file will serve as a starting point for introducing static typing.

2. Enable TypeScript Compiler

Ensure that you have TypeScript installed and a tsconfig.json configuration file set up in your project. The tsconfig.json file allows you to specify compiler options and control how TypeScript compiles your code.

3. Rename JavaScript Files

To distinguish between JavaScript and TypeScript files, consider renaming your existing JavaScript files with a .js extension to .ts. This step is optional but can help keep track of your migration progress.

4. Incremental Type Annotations

Begin adding type annotations to variables, function parameters, and return values in the TypeScript file you created. TypeScript's type inference will help you identify and address type issues. Focus on the areas of your code where type safety is most critical.

5. Handle Dependencies

If your code relies on external JavaScript libraries, you may need to find or create type definitions (.d.ts files) for these libraries. TypeScript can provide better type checking and code intelligence when type definitions are available.

6. Test and Validate

As you add type annotations and make changes, it's crucial to test your code thoroughly. Write unit tests and run them using a testing framework like Jest or Mocha. This helps ensure that your code behaves correctly and that type-related issues are caught early.

7. Linter Integration

Integrate a linter such as ESLint or TSLint into your project. Linters can help enforce coding standards and catch potential issues, including type-related errors.

8. Convert More Files

Continue the migration process by selecting additional JavaScript files or modules to convert to TypeScript. Follow the same steps of adding type annotations, handling dependencies, and testing. Repeat this process iteratively until your entire codebase is migrated.

9. Use Type Definitions

Take advantage of TypeScript's type system to improve code quality and maintainability. Leverage interfaces, enums, custom types, and type aliases to create expressive and precise type definitions.

10. Refactor as Needed

As you migrate your code to TypeScript, you may encounter opportunities for refactoring and improving your codebase. Consider refactoring for clarity, maintainability, and performance.

11. Code Review and Collaboration

Involve your team members in the migration process. Code reviews and collaboration can help identify issues, share knowledge, and ensure that best practices are followed.

12. Continuous Integration

Integrate TypeScript into your continuous integration (CI) pipeline to ensure that your code is type-checked and compiled as part of the build process. This helps catch issues early and prevents TypeScript-related regressions.

13. Documentation

Update your project's documentation to reflect the use of TypeScript. Provide information on TypeScript-specific features, conventions, and any custom type definitions used in your codebase.

14. Monitor and Maintain

After completing the migration, continue to monitor and maintain your TypeScript codebase. TypeScript evolves, and new features and best practices may emerge. Stay up-to-date to take full advantage of TypeScript's capabilities.

By following this step-by-step migration process, you can efficiently transition from JavaScript to TypeScript while maintaining code quality and minimizing disruption to your development workflow.

4.3 Handling Common Migration Challenges

Migrating from JavaScript to TypeScript can present various challenges, but with proper strategies and awareness, you can overcome them. In this section, we'll address some common challenges that developers often face during the migration process and provide solutions.

1. Dealing with Unannotated Dependencies

When migrating a JavaScript codebase, you may encounter external libraries or modules without type definitions. This can hinder TypeScript's type checking. To address this:

- Search for existing type definitions on DefinitelyTyped or other community repositories.

- Create your own type definitions in a .d.ts file when necessary.

- Use the any type sparingly to interface with untyped JavaScript code temporarily.

2. Implicit Any Errors

TypeScript's —noImplicitAny flag helps catch variables with implicit any types. However, in large codebases, enabling this flag can lead to numerous errors. To handle this:

- Gradually enable —noImplicitAny in your TypeScript configuration to identify and fix implicit any issues incrementally.

- Annotate function return types and parameters to provide type information.

3. Strict Null Checks

Enabling —strictNullChecks can surface issues related to null and undefined. To manage this:

- Use the null and undefined union types (| null | undefined) for variables that can have these values.

- Leverage optional properties using the ? syntax (e.g., property?: string) to indicate optional values.

- Consider using non-null assertion operators (!) when you're certain that a value is not null or undefined.

4. Handling Existing Bugs

Migrating to TypeScript may reveal existing bugs in your code that were previously unnoticed. To address this:

- Treat bug fixing as an essential part of the migration process. Correct issues as you encounter them.

- Write comprehensive unit tests to catch regressions and ensure the correctness of your code.

5. Maintaining Build Configuration

Integrating TypeScript into your existing build process can be challenging. To manage this:

- Update your build tools (e.g., Webpack, Babel) to support TypeScript.

- Ensure your TypeScript configuration (tsconfig.json) aligns with your build setup.

- Configure your build pipeline to transpile TypeScript code into JavaScript.

6. Collaborating with a Team

Migrating a project to TypeScript is more manageable with team collaboration. To facilitate this:

- Communicate with team members about the migration plan and its benefits.

- Establish coding standards and guidelines for TypeScript usage.

- Conduct code reviews to ensure TypeScript best practices are followed.

7. Balancing Migration Speed

Deciding the pace of migration is essential. To balance migration speed:

- Consider your project's size and deadlines. A slower migration might be necessary for larger codebases.

- Prioritize critical components and high-risk areas for migration first.

- Use tools like TypeScript's incremental compilation to speed up the process.

8. Learning TypeScript

If your team is unfamiliar with TypeScript, invest time in learning its features and best practices. You can:

- Provide training sessions or access to learning resources.

- Encourage team members to explore TypeScript gradually.

- Use online documentation and TypeScript community forums for guidance.

9. Gradual Refactoring

Migrating to TypeScript is an opportunity to refactor and improve your codebase. To manage this:

- Identify code smells and refactoring opportunities during the migration process.

- Prioritize code quality alongside the introduction of types.

10. Monitoring for Regressions

After migration, monitor your application for regressions and issues. Maintain a robust testing and validation process to ensure that TypeScript changes do not introduce new problems.

By addressing these common challenges and adopting best practices, you can successfully navigate the migration from JavaScript to TypeScript and enjoy the benefits of a statically typed codebase.

4.4 Leveraging TypeScript in Existing Projects

Integrating TypeScript into an existing JavaScript project is a valuable step to enhance code quality, maintainability, and developer productivity. In this section, we'll explore strategies and best practices for effectively leveraging TypeScript in your ongoing projects.

1. Gradual Adoption

One of the strengths of TypeScript is its compatibility with JavaScript. You can introduce TypeScript incrementally into your project without rewriting all the code. Start by converting specific modules or files to TypeScript while leaving the rest as JavaScript. This allows you to experience the benefits of TypeScript gradually.

2. tsconfig.json Configuration

A well-configured tsconfig.json file is essential for TypeScript integration. Ensure that the configuration aligns with your project's needs and build setup. You can customize TypeScript options such as module resolution, output directory, target JavaScript version, and strictness according to your project's requirements.

3. Type Definitions

In an existing project, you may rely on external libraries that lack official type definitions. TypeScript's type system shines when you have precise type information. Consider these options:

- Search for community-contributed type definitions on DefinitelyTyped.

- Create your own type definitions (.d.ts files) for libraries that don't have existing type definitions.

- Use the any type to temporarily interact with untyped JavaScript code, but aim to add type definitions when possible.

4. Custom Types

Leverage TypeScript's ability to define custom types, interfaces, and type aliases to enhance code readability and maintainability. Create types that accurately represent the data structures and domain concepts in your project. Well-defined types can serve as documentation and reduce the risk of runtime errors.

5. Type Annotations

Introduce type annotations gradually by annotating variables, function parameters, and return values. TypeScript's type inference can help identify types, but explicit annotations improve code clarity and enable TypeScript to catch more issues.

6. Linting and Code Analysis

Integrate a TypeScript-aware linter such as ESLint with the @typescript-eslint plugin or TSLint (deprecated) into your project. Linters can enforce coding standards and catch TypeScript-related issues early in the development process.

7. Testing and Validation

Thoroughly test your code as you introduce TypeScript. Write unit tests to validate the behavior of TypeScript-annotated functions and components. Consider using testing libraries like Jest, Mocha, or Jasmine for automated testing.

8. Code Reviews and Collaboration

Collaborate with team members during the TypeScript adoption process. Conduct code reviews to ensure that TypeScript best practices are followed, and team members understand how to work with TypeScript.

9. Documentation

Update your project's documentation to include information on TypeScript usage. Document custom types, interfaces, and any TypeScript-specific patterns used in your codebase. This helps new team members and contributors understand your project.

10. Continuous Integration

Include TypeScript type checking and compilation as part of your continuous integration (CI) pipeline. Ensure that TypeScript errors are caught early in the development process, preventing TypeScript-related regressions.

11. Refactoring Opportunities

As you introduce TypeScript, you may discover opportunities for code refactoring. Take advantage of TypeScript's static analysis to improve code quality, eliminate duplication, and enhance maintainability.

12. Monitoring and Maintenance

After TypeScript integration, continue to monitor and maintain your project. Stay up-to-date with TypeScript updates, new features, and best practices. Regularly review and refactor your TypeScript code to keep it clean and efficient.

Leveraging TypeScript in an existing JavaScript project is a rewarding endeavor that enhances code quality and developer productivity. By following these best practices and gradually adopting TypeScript, you can successfully integrate it into your ongoing projects.

4.5 Post-migration Best Practices

After successfully migrating from JavaScript to TypeScript, it's crucial to maintain and optimize your TypeScript codebase. In this section, we'll explore post-migration best practices to ensure that your project continues to benefit from TypeScript's features.

1. Type Coverage

Maintaining high type coverage is essential to reap the benefits of TypeScript fully. Use tools like TSLint or ESLint with TypeScript rules to enforce type checking across your codebase. Aim to minimize the usage of the any type, as it reduces the effectiveness of TypeScript's static analysis.

2. Continuous Integration (CI)

Integrate TypeScript checks into your continuous integration (CI) pipeline. Ensure that every pull request or code commit undergoes TypeScript type checking and compilation. This practice prevents TypeScript-related regressions and enforces code quality.

3. Code Reviews

Continue to conduct code reviews with an emphasis on TypeScript code quality. Collaborate with team members to identify areas for improvement, adherence to TypeScript best practices, and opportunities for refactoring.

4. Version Control

Use version control effectively to track changes and updates to your TypeScript code. Make use of descriptive commit messages and follow branching strategies that align with your team's workflow. This helps in maintaining a well-organized codebase.

5. Documentation

Keep your TypeScript codebase well-documented. Document custom types, interfaces, and significant modules or components. This documentation helps developers understand the structure of your code and how to work with TypeScript-specific patterns.

6. Type Definitions

Regularly update type definitions for external libraries and dependencies. As libraries evolve, new versions may introduce breaking changes or enhancements. Keeping type definitions up-to-date ensures a smooth development experience.

7. TypeScript Updates

Stay informed about TypeScript updates and new features. TypeScript evolves continuously, and new versions may introduce improvements and optimizations. Updating to the latest TypeScript version helps you take advantage of these enhancements.

8. Performance Optimization

Optimize your TypeScript code for performance as needed. Profile and benchmark your application to identify bottlenecks. Utilize TypeScript's type system to catch performance-related issues early in development.

9. Error Handling

Continue to focus on error handling and validation. TypeScript's type system can help catch potential error sources during development. Create custom types for error handling scenarios and use TypeScript's type inference to improve error checks.

10. Refactoring

Embrace the opportunity for ongoing refactoring. As your project evolves, refactor code to maintain code quality, readability, and adherence to TypeScript best practices. Eliminate redundant code and ensure consistency across your codebase.

11. Monitoring and Maintenance

Establish practices for monitoring and maintaining your TypeScript codebase over time. Regularly review and assess the codebase for code smells, maintainability, and performance. Use code analysis tools to catch issues and enforce code quality.

12. Training and Knowledge Sharing

Continue to invest in team training and knowledge sharing related to TypeScript. Share best practices, tips, and experiences among team members to improve TypeScript adoption and proficiency.

13. Community Engagement

Participate in the TypeScript community by attending meetups, conferences, and online forums. Engaging with the community can provide valuable insights, solutions to challenges, and opportunities to share your knowledge.

14. Cross-team Collaboration

Collaborate with other teams or projects within your organization that use TypeScript. Sharing experiences and knowledge can lead to standardized practices and improved TypeScript adoption across the organization.

By following these post-migration best practices, you can ensure that your TypeScript codebase remains robust, maintainable, and aligned with industry standards. TypeScript's static type checking and tooling will continue to enhance your development experience and contribute to code quality.

Chapter 5: Type Safety and Error Handling

5.1 The Importance of Type Safety

Type safety is a fundamental concept in software development, and it plays a crucial role in building reliable and maintainable applications. In this section, we'll explore the significance of type safety in programming and how TypeScript helps ensure it.

What Is Type Safety?

Type safety, also known as type correctness or type soundness, refers to the property of a programming language or system that prevents unintended or illegal operations on data. In a type-safe environment, the compiler or runtime system enforces strict adherence to the data types defined in the program.

Benefits of Type Safety

Type safety offers several advantages in software development:

1. **Preventing Type Errors**: Type-safe languages catch type errors at compile-time or runtime, reducing the likelihood of runtime crashes and unexpected behavior caused by type mismatches.
2. **Code Readability and Maintainability**: Type annotations make code more self-explanatory and provide documentation about the data's intended usage, improving code readability. This aids in maintenance and collaboration among developers.
3. **Refactoring Confidence**: When refactoring code or making changes to existing code, type safety provides

confidence that changes won't introduce subtle bugs or type-related issues.

4. **Tooling Support**: Type-safe languages benefit from powerful development tools, such as intelligent code editors, auto-completion, and integrated debugging, which can significantly enhance developer productivity.

TypeScript and Type Safety

TypeScript, as a statically typed superset of JavaScript, brings type safety to the JavaScript ecosystem. It offers the following features to ensure type safety:

1. **Static Type Checking**: TypeScript performs type checking at compile-time, catching type errors before the code is executed. This eliminates a large class of runtime errors.
2. **Type Annotations**: TypeScript allows developers to add type annotations to variables, function parameters, and return values, providing explicit type information and enabling the compiler to perform rigorous type checking.
3. **Type Inference**: TypeScript's type inference automatically deduces types when type annotations are not provided. This reduces the need for redundant type annotations while maintaining type safety.
4. **Custom Types**: TypeScript supports the creation of custom types, interfaces, enums, and type aliases, enabling developers to define precise data structures and domain-specific types.
5. **Union and Intersection Types**: TypeScript offers union types (e.g., number | string) and intersection types (e.g., Person & Address) to model complex data scenarios accurately.
6. **Nullable Types**: TypeScript's strictNullChecks flag helps

avoid null and undefined errors by making nullable types explicit.

7. **Type Guards and Assertion**: TypeScript provides mechanisms like type guards and type assertions to work with types dynamically and safely.

In summary, type safety is a critical aspect of software development, as it helps catch errors early, enhances code readability, and improves code maintainability. TypeScript, with its static type checking and type system features, empowers developers to build type-safe applications in the JavaScript ecosystem.

5.2 Strategies for Effective Error Handling

Error handling is an essential aspect of software development, ensuring that applications can gracefully respond to unexpected situations or issues. In TypeScript, effective error handling is facilitated by the language's strong typing and type safety features. In this section, we'll explore strategies and best practices for handling errors in TypeScript.

1. Use Explicit Error Types

One of TypeScript's strengths is its ability to define custom error types using classes or type aliases. When defining errors explicitly, you provide better documentation and make it clear what kinds of errors can occur in your code. Here's an example of creating a custom error class:

```typescript
class CustomError extends Error {

constructor(message: string) {

super(message);
```

```typescript
this.name = 'CustomError';

}

}

// Usage

try {

// Code that may throw a CustomError

} catch (error) {

if (error instanceof CustomError) {

// Handle the CustomError

} else {

// Handle other errors or rethrow

throw error;

}

}
```

2. Avoid Using Generic any Type

While TypeScript allows you to use the any type for flexibility, it's best to avoid it for error handling. Using any can weaken type safety and make it harder to catch errors at compile-time. Instead, use specific error types or union types to represent potential error scenarios.

3. Use Union Types for Multiple Error Types

In many cases, a function or operation may encounter multiple types of errors. TypeScript's union types are handy for representing such scenarios. For instance, you can define an error type that can be either a network error or a file system error:

```typescript
type NetworkError = { type: 'network'; message: string };

type FileSystemError = { type: 'filesystem'; message: string };

type AppError = NetworkError | FileSystemError;

function handleError(error: AppError) {

switch (error.type) {

case 'network':

console.error('Network error:', error.message);

break;

case 'filesystem':

console.error('File system error:', error.message);

break;

}

}
```

4. Use try...catch Blocks

The try...catch statement allows you to handle exceptions gracefully. In TypeScript, you can catch specific error types and handle them appropriately. Be sure to provide meaningful error messages to aid in debugging:

```typescript
try {

// Code that may throw an error

} catch (error) {

if (error instanceof CustomError) {

console.error('Custom error occurred:', error.message);

} else {

console.error('An unknown error occurred:', error);

}

}
```

5. Propagate Errors with throw

When handling errors in functions, consider whether it's appropriate to propagate the error to the calling code using the throw statement. Propagating errors allows higher-level code to handle errors or make decisions based on the error information.

```typescript
function divide(a: number, b: number): number {

if (b === 0) {

throw new Error('Division by zero is not allowed.');

}

return a / b;

}
```

6. Use Promises and async/await

When working with asynchronous code, use Promises and async/await for error handling. Promises allow you to handle both resolved and rejected states, making it clear when an operation can result in an error. Here's an example:

async function fetchData() {

try {

const response = **await** fetch('https://example.com/data.json');

if (!response.ok) {

throw new Error('Failed to fetch data');

}

const data = **await** response.json();

return data;

} **catch** (error) {

console.error('Error fetching data:', error);

throw error; // *Propagate the error*

}

}

7. Logging and Reporting

Implement robust logging and error reporting mechanisms in your applications. Proper logging helps diagnose issues in production and provides insights into error patterns. Tools like Winston, Bunyan, or built-in logging in Node.js can be useful for this purpose.

8. Error Boundaries in UI Libraries

If you're building user interfaces with libraries like React, consider implementing error boundaries to isolate and handle UI-related errors gracefully without crashing the entire application. React's ErrorBoundary component is a good example.

In TypeScript, effective error handling is enhanced by the language's type safety features, which enable you to create explicit error types and handle errors with precision. By following these best practices, you can improve the robustness and reliability of your TypeScript applications.

5.3 Utilizing TypeScript for Better Debugging

Debugging is an integral part of the software development process, and TypeScript offers features that can significantly improve the debugging experience. In this section, we'll explore how TypeScript aids in debugging and provides tools and techniques to catch and resolve issues effectively.

1. Static Type Checking

TypeScript's static type checking catches many potential issues during development, even before the code is executed. This early error detection reduces the number of runtime errors and makes debugging more focused on logic and business-related problems rather than type mismatches.

For example, if you attempt to assign a string to a variable that should hold a number, TypeScript will flag it as a type error during development, preventing the need to debug such issues at runtime.

2. Enhanced Code Editors

Modern code editors like Visual Studio Code (VS Code) provide excellent support for TypeScript. Features like auto-completion, intelligent code suggestions, and real-time error highlighting make it easier to spot and fix issues as you write code.

The integrated development environment (IDE) also offers a powerful debugging experience with breakpoints, step-through execution, and variable inspection, making it convenient to track down and resolve problems.

3. Strong Typing for Function Signatures

TypeScript allows you to define clear and robust function signatures, including parameter types and return types. This not only improves code documentation but also helps with debugging by providing meaningful information about what a function expects and returns.

Consider this function with explicit typing:

```
function calculateTotal(price: number, quantity: number): number {

return price * quantity;

}
```

With such type annotations, the IDE can provide insights into the expected types of arguments and the return value, reducing the chances of passing incorrect values and making debugging more straightforward.

4. Null and Undefined Checks

TypeScript's strictNullChecks flag ensures that you handle potential null and undefined values explicitly. By addressing these cases in your code, you can prevent common runtime errors, such as "Cannot read property 'something' of undefined." This flag encourages safe coding practices and leads to fewer debugging sessions caused by unexpected null or undefined values.

5. Custom Error Types

As mentioned in previous sections, TypeScript allows you to define custom error types using classes or type aliases. Utilizing custom error types can make it easier to identify specific error scenarios and handle them gracefully during debugging.

```typescript
class CustomError extends Error {

constructor(message: string) {

super(message);

this.name = 'CustomError';

}

}
```

By throwing and catching custom error types, you can distinguish between different error situations and take appropriate debugging measures.

6. Debugging with console.log

While advanced debugging tools are valuable, sometimes the simplest method is the most effective. TypeScript, like JavaScript, allows you to use console.log statements strategically to inspect variables, values, and control flow during development. It's a quick way to gain insights into your code's behavior.

```typescript
function calculateTotal(price: number, quantity: number): number {

console.log('Calculating total...');

console.log('Price:', price);

console.log('Quantity:', quantity);

const total = price * quantity;

console.log('Total:', total);

return total;

}
```

7. Debugging in TypeScript Playground

For experimentation and learning purposes, TypeScript offers an online tool called TypeScript Playground. It's an interactive editor that allows you to write TypeScript code and see the resulting JavaScript output. It's a useful environment for debugging and exploring TypeScript features.

8. Leveraging Source Maps

When TypeScript code is transpiled to JavaScript, source maps are generated. These maps provide a mapping between the JavaScript code and the original TypeScript code. When debugging in a browser or other runtime environment, source maps allow you to see and debug the original TypeScript code, making it easier to understand and fix issues.

In conclusion, TypeScript enhances the debugging process by catching errors early through static type checking, offering robust type annotations for function signatures, and providing strong tooling support in modern code editors. Custom error types, strict null checks, and strategic use of console.log further contribute to efficient debugging. Leveraging TypeScript's features and tools, developers can streamline the debugging process and build more reliable applications.

5.4 Creating Custom Types for Error Handling

Custom error types are a powerful tool in TypeScript for improving error handling and ensuring that your codebase remains robust. In this section, we'll delve into creating custom error types and explore how they can enhance error management in TypeScript applications.

1. Benefits of Custom Error Types

Custom error types provide several advantages:

- **Clarity**: They make error scenarios explicit, which enhances code readability and makes it easier to understand how different errors are handled.

- **Consistency**: By defining standardized error types across your codebase, you ensure a consistent approach to error management, making it easier for developers to work with and maintain the code.

- **Type Safety**: Custom error types are statically typed, ensuring that you handle errors in a type-safe manner, reducing the risk of runtime errors.

- **Documentation**: Custom error types serve as documentation, providing insights into potential error scenarios and how to handle them.

2. Creating a Custom Error Type

To create a custom error type in TypeScript, you can define a new error class that extends the built-in Error class. Here's an example:

```
class CustomError extends Error {

constructor(message: string) {

super(message);

this.name = 'CustomError';

}

}
```

In this example, CustomError is a subclass of Error with a custom constructor that allows you to set the error message and name.

3. Throwing Custom Errors

You can throw instances of your custom error type using the throw statement. This allows you to raise specific errors when certain conditions are met. For instance:

```
function validateInput(input: string) {

if (!input) {
```

```typescript
throw new CustomError('Input is required.');

}

}
```

4. Handling Custom Errors

When you catch errors, you can use TypeScript's type checking to handle custom errors specifically while catching other errors more generally. Here's an example:

```typescript
try {

// Code that may throw a custom error

} catch (error) {

if (error instanceof CustomError) {

console.error('Custom error occurred:', error.message);

// Handle the custom error

} else {

console.error('An unknown error occurred:', error);

// Handle other errors or rethrow

throw error;

}

}
```

5. Additional Properties

You can extend your custom error type by adding additional properties that provide context about the error. For example, you might include an error code or extra details that aid in debugging:

```
class CustomError extends Error {

code: number;

constructor(message: string, code: number) {

super(message);

this.name = 'CustomError';

this.code = code;

}

}

// Usage

try {

// Code that may throw a custom error

} catch (error) {

if (error instanceof CustomError) {

console.error('Custom error occurred:', error.message);

console.error('Error code:', error.code);

// Handle the custom error

} else {
```

```
console.error('An unknown error occurred:', error);

// Handle other errors or rethrow

throw error;

}

}
```

6. Hierarchical Error Types

In more complex applications, you may want to create a hierarchy of custom error types to represent different error categories or levels. This allows you to handle errors at different levels of granularity.

```
class NetworkError extends CustomError {

constructor(message: string, code: number) {

super(message, code);

this.name = 'NetworkError';

}

}

class DatabaseError extends CustomError {

constructor(message: string, code: number) {

super(message, code);

this.name = 'DatabaseError';

}

}
```

```typescript
// Usage

try {

// Code that may throw a network or database error

} catch (error) {

if (error instanceof NetworkError) {

console.error('Network error occurred:', error.message);

// Handle the network error

} else if (error instanceof DatabaseError) {

console.error('Database error occurred:', error.message);

// Handle the database error

} else {

console.error('An unknown error occurred:', error);

// Handle other errors or rethrow

throw error;

}

}
```

Custom error types in TypeScript provide a powerful way to manage and communicate errors in your code. By defining specific error types and using TypeScript's type checking capabilities, you can create more reliable and maintainable error-handling code. Additionally, custom errors enhance code documentation and make error scenarios explicit, improving overall code quality.

5.5 Practical Examples of Error Handling in TypeScript

To understand error handling in TypeScript better, let's explore some practical examples that demonstrate how to handle various types of errors effectively. Error handling is a critical aspect of writing robust applications, and TypeScript's strong typing and custom error types can help achieve this goal.

1. Handling Asynchronous Errors

Asynchronous operations, such as fetching data from an API or reading a file, can result in errors. In TypeScript, handling such errors typically involves using Promises and the async/await syntax.

```typescript
async function fetchData() {

try {

const response = await fetch('https://example.com/data.json');

if (!response.ok) {

throw new Error('Failed to fetch data');

}

const data = await response.json();

return data;

} catch (error) {

console.error('Error fetching data:', error.message);

throw error; // Propagate the error

}
```

```
}
```

In this example, we use async/await to make an HTTP request. If the response is not successful, we throw a custom error. Any errors encountered during the operation are caught and logged, and then rethrown for further handling.

2. Validating User Input

Input validation is crucial for ensuring the correctness and security of user-provided data. TypeScript's type system can help with validation by enforcing the expected data types.

```typescript
function validateEmail(email: string): void {

if (!/^[A-Z0-9._%+-]+@[A-Z0-9.-]+\.[A-Z]{2,}$/i.test(email)) {

throw new CustomError('Invalid email address');

}

}

try {

const userInput = 'invalid-email';

validateEmail(userInput);

} catch (error) {

if (error instanceof CustomError) {

console.error('Invalid input:', error.message);

// Handle the custom error

} else {
```

```
console.error('An unknown error occurred:', error);
```

// Handle other errors or rethrow

```
throw error;
```

```
}
```

```
}
```

In this example, we define a validateEmail function that checks if the provided email address is valid. If it's not valid, we throw a custom error. The error is then caught and handled appropriately.

3. Dealing with File I/O Errors

When working with files, errors can occur due to various reasons, such as missing files, permissions, or disk issues. TypeScript can help us handle these errors gracefully.

```
import { promises as fs } from 'fs';
```

```
async function readFile(filePath: string): Promise<string> {
```

```
try {
```

```
const fileContent = await fs.readFile(filePath, 'utf-8');
```

```
return fileContent;
```

```
} catch (error) {
```

```
console.error(`Error reading file at ${filePath}:`, error.message);
```

```
throw error; // Propagate the error
```

```
}
```

```
}
```

In this code, we use Node.js's fs.promises.readFile function to read a file asynchronously. If an error occurs, such as the file not being found, we catch the error and log it, then rethrow it for further handling.

4. Handling Network Errors

When making network requests, errors can happen due to network issues, timeouts, or incorrect URLs. TypeScript allows us to handle these scenarios effectively.

```typescript
import axios from 'axios';

async function fetchUserData(userId: number): Promise<User | null> {

try {

const response = await axios.get(`https://api.example.com/user/${userId}`);

if (response.status !== 200) {

throw new CustomError('Failed to fetch user data');

}

return response.data as User;

} catch (error) {

console.error('Error fetching user data:', error.message);

throw error; // Propagate the error

}

}
```

In this example, we use the Axios library for making HTTP requests. If the response status is not 200 (OK), we throw a custom error. Any network errors are caught and logged, and then rethrown for handling.

These practical examples demonstrate how TypeScript can be used to handle different types of errors in real-world scenarios. By leveraging TypeScript's type system and custom error types, you can write code that is not only more robust but also easier to understand and maintain. Effective error handling is essential for delivering reliable software.

Chapter 6: Working with Libraries and Frameworks

6.1 Integrating TypeScript with Popular JavaScript Libraries

Integrating TypeScript with existing JavaScript libraries is a common scenario in modern web development. Many popular libraries and frameworks, such as React, Angular, and Vue, have TypeScript support to enhance type safety and developer productivity. In this section, we will explore how to integrate TypeScript into some of these libraries and best practices for a smooth development experience.

1. TypeScript and React

React is a widely used JavaScript library for building user interfaces. TypeScript provides excellent support for React, allowing you to write type-safe components and enhance code quality. To get started with TypeScript in React:

 # Create a new React app with TypeScript template

npx create-react-app my-app—template typescript

This command sets up a new React project with TypeScript configuration. You can now create React components with TypeScript, taking advantage of type inference and autocompletion.

2. TypeScript and Angular

Angular is a comprehensive web application framework developed by Google. Angular has built-in support for TypeScript, making it a natural choice for developers who prefer strong typing. To create an Angular project with TypeScript:

 # Install Angular CLI globally

npm install -g @angular/cli

 # Create a new Angular project

ng new my-angular-app

Follow the prompts to configure your project, and Angular CLI will generate a TypeScript-based Angular application for you. You can then use TypeScript to define components, services, and other parts of your Angular app.

3. TypeScript and Vue

Vue is a progressive JavaScript framework for building user interfaces. While Vue is often associated with JavaScript, you can seamlessly use TypeScript with Vue as well. To set up a Vue project with TypeScript:

 # Create a new Vue project with Vue CLI

npm install -g @vue/cli

vue create my-vue-app

During the Vue project setup process, you can choose to use TypeScript as a language preset. Selecting TypeScript will configure your Vue project to use TypeScript for single-file components and other parts of your application.

4. Type Definitions for Libraries

When integrating TypeScript with JavaScript libraries, you may need type definitions (typings) to provide type information for the library's API. Many popular libraries have community-contributed type definitions available on DefinitelyTyped (https://definitelytyped.org/). You can install these type definitions using npm or yarn.

For example, to install type definitions for the lodash library:

 # Install lodash and its type definitions

npm install lodash

npm install @types/lodash—save-dev

By installing the corresponding type definitions, you enable TypeScript to provide type checking and autocompletion for the library.

5. Custom Type Declarations

In some cases, you may need to write custom type declarations for libraries that don't have official type definitions. TypeScript allows you to declare the types for external modules using declaration files (.d.ts). For example:

// custom.d.ts

declare module 'my-library' {

export function doSomething(): void;

}

You can then use the doSomething function from 'my-library' in your TypeScript code.

Integrating TypeScript with JavaScript libraries and frameworks offers the benefits of type safety and enhanced tooling support. Whether you're working with React, Angular, Vue, or other libraries, TypeScript can help you write more reliable and maintainable code.

6.2 TypeScript with Front-end Frameworks (React, Angular, Vue)

Front-end frameworks like React, Angular, and Vue have gained immense popularity in web development due to their ability to simplify the creation of complex user interfaces. TypeScript can be seamlessly integrated with these frameworks, offering developers the advantages of static typing and improved developer tooling. In this section, we will explore how TypeScript works with each of these front-end frameworks.

TypeScript in React

React is a JavaScript library for building user interfaces, and TypeScript is an excellent choice for enhancing type safety in React applications. To get started with TypeScript in React, you can create a new React project with TypeScript using the following command:

```
npx create-react-app my-app—template typescript
```

This command sets up a new React project with TypeScript configuration. With TypeScript, you can define type interfaces for props and states, ensuring that your components receive the correct data types. Here's an example of a TypeScript component in React:

```
import React, { FC } from 'react';
```

```
interface Props {

name: string;

}

const Greeting: FC<Props> = ({ name }) => {

return <div>Hello, {name}!</div>;

};

export default Greeting;
```

By defining the Props interface and specifying it as the generic type for FC (functional component), TypeScript helps catch type errors during development and provides better auto-completion.

TypeScript in Angular

Angular is a comprehensive web application framework developed by Google. TypeScript is the primary language used for Angular development, making it a powerful combination for building large-scale web applications. To create an Angular project with TypeScript, you can use the Angular CLI:

```
npm install -g @angular/cli

ng new my-angular-app
```

During the project setup, you can choose TypeScript as the default language. Angular's dependency injection and strong typing work seamlessly with TypeScript, enabling you to create maintainable and scalable applications.

TypeScript in Vue

Vue is a progressive JavaScript framework for building user interfaces. While Vue is often associated with JavaScript, TypeScript can be used with Vue projects to provide type checking and improved development experiences. To set up a Vue project with TypeScript, you can use the Vue CLI:

npm install -g @vue/cli

vue create my-vue-app

During the Vue project setup process, you can choose TypeScript as a language preset. This configures your Vue project to use TypeScript for single-file components and other parts of your application. Here's an example of a TypeScript-based Vue component:

```
<template>

<div>

<p>{{ message }}</p>

</div>

</template>

<script lang="ts">

import { Vue, Component } from 'vue-property-decorator';

@Component

export default class HelloWorld extends Vue {

private message: string = 'Hello, Vue!';

}
```

```
</script>
```

In this example, we use TypeScript decorators and type annotations to define a Vue component with type safety.

Benefits of TypeScript with Front-end Frameworks

Integrating TypeScript with front-end frameworks offers several benefits:

1. **Type Safety**: TypeScript helps catch type-related errors during development, reducing runtime issues.
2. **Enhanced Tooling**: IDEs provide better auto-completion, navigation, and refactoring support with TypeScript.
3. **Improved Maintainability**: Strong typing makes code more self-documenting and easier to understand, enhancing code maintainability.
4. **Large-scale Application Support**: TypeScript's static typing is particularly valuable in large-scale applications, where maintaining code quality is crucial.
5. **Community and Ecosystem**: TypeScript has a strong community and an ecosystem of libraries and tools that support front-end development.

By leveraging TypeScript's capabilities, you can write more reliable and maintainable front-end code while using your preferred framework—React, Angular, or Vue.

6.3 Managing Types in Third-party Libraries

When developing applications with TypeScript, you often need to interact with third-party libraries and packages that may not have built-in TypeScript support. In this section, we'll explore strategies for managing types in such situations, allowing you to leverage

TypeScript's benefits even when working with external JavaScript libraries.

1. Using Declaration Files

Declaration files (also known as .d.ts files) provide type information for JavaScript libraries that don't have native TypeScript support. These files declare the types and interfaces used by the library, allowing TypeScript to perform type checking and provide IntelliSense.

To use a declaration file, you typically install it alongside the library. For example, if you're using the lodash library, you can install its corresponding declaration file as follows:

npm install lodash @types/lodash—save

In this example, @types/lodash is the declaration file for lodash. Once installed, you can import and use lodash functions with type safety:

import * **as _ from** 'lodash';

const result: number = _.add(5, 3); // *TypeScript knows that the result is a number*

Many popular libraries have community-maintained declaration files available on DefinitelyTyped (https://definitelytyped.org/). You can search for declaration files for your desired library and install them as needed.

2. Type Assertion

Type assertion (also known as type casting) allows you to tell TypeScript that you know more about the type of a value than it does. While it should be used with caution, it can be handy when working with external libraries that TypeScript can't infer types for.

Here's an example of type assertion:

const someValue: any = 'Hello, TypeScript!';

const strLength: number = (someValue **as** string).length; // *Type assertion*

In this example, someValue is initially of type any, but we use type assertion to tell TypeScript that it should be treated as a string. This allows us to access the length property without type errors.

3. Writing Custom Type Definitions

If a library doesn't have a suitable declaration file, you can write your own custom type definitions in a .d.ts file. TypeScript will automatically pick up these declarations when you include them in your project.

Here's an example of a custom type definition for a fictional library 'my-library':

// *custom.d.ts*

declare module 'my-library' {

export function doSomething(): void;

export function calculate(x: number, y: number): number;

}

Now, you can import and use 'my-library' in your TypeScript code with type safety:

```typescript
import * as myLib from 'my-library';

myLib.doSomething(); // Type-checked call

const result: number = myLib.calculate(5, 3); // Type-checked call
```

Writing custom type definitions can be particularly useful when you have control over the library's API but no official declaration file is available.

4. DefinitelyTyped Repository

The DefinitelyTyped repository (https://github.com/DefinitelyTyped/DefinitelyTyped) is a community-driven effort to provide type definitions for popular JavaScript libraries. You can contribute by submitting type definition files for libraries you use or benefit from existing contributions.

5. Dynamically Typed Libraries

In some cases, you may encounter JavaScript libraries that are dynamically typed and don't provide static type information. While TypeScript can't perform full type checking in these situations, you can still benefit from TypeScript's features like improved tooling and IntelliSense. Use type assertion or custom type declarations as necessary to provide some level of type safety.

Managing types in third-party libraries is essential for leveraging TypeScript's advantages in your projects. Whether you're using declaration files, type assertion, or writing custom type definitions, TypeScript provides flexible options to work with JavaScript libraries effectively and safely.

6.4 Building Custom Libraries with

TypeScript

Building custom libraries with TypeScript is a powerful way to encapsulate functionality, promote code reuse, and ensure type safety across projects. In this section, we will explore the process of creating custom libraries using TypeScript, including best practices and considerations.

1. Setting Up a TypeScript Library Project

To create a custom TypeScript library, you can use a tool like npm or yarn to initialize a new TypeScript project. Here's how to set up a basic library project structure:

```
# Create a new directory for your library

mkdir my-ts-library

cd my-ts-library

# Initialize a new TypeScript project

npm init -y

# Install TypeScript as a development dependency

npm install typescript—save-dev

# Create a 'src' directory for your library source code

mkdir src

# Create a TypeScript file for your library code

touch src/myLibrary.ts
```

Now, you have a basic project structure with a TypeScript source file (e.g., myLibrary.ts) inside the src directory.

2. Writing Library Code

In your myLibrary.ts file, you can start writing your library code. Export functions, classes, or modules that you want to make available to users of your library. Here's an example of a simple library with a function that adds two numbers:

// src/myLibrary.ts

export function addNumbers(x: number, y: number): number {

return x + y;

}

3. Configuring TypeScript

To configure TypeScript for your library project, create a tsconfig.json file in the project root. You can use the TypeScript CLI to initialize a basic tsconfig.json file:

npx tsc—init

You can then customize the tsconfig.json file to match your project's requirements. For a library, make sure to set the "declaration" option to true. This tells TypeScript to generate declaration files (.d.ts) alongside your JavaScript files, enabling users of your library to benefit from type checking.

4. Generating Declaration Files

To generate declaration files for your library, you can run the TypeScript compiler (tsc) with the —declaration flag:

npx tsc—declaration

This command compiles your TypeScript code and generates corresponding declaration files in the dist directory. Users of your library can then import your library and take advantage of type checking in their projects.

5. Publishing Your Library

To make your library available to others, you can publish it to the npm registry. Ensure that you have an npm account and run the following commands in your library project:

 # Log in to your npm account

npm login

 # Publish your library

npm publish

Your library is now published on npm, and others can install and use it in their projects using npm install.

6. Consuming Your Library

Users can consume your TypeScript library in their projects just like any other npm package. They can install it using npm install, and TypeScript will automatically provide type information from the generated declaration files.

 # Install your library as a dependency

npm install my-ts-library

 # Import and use your library in their TypeScript code

import { addNumbers } from 'my-ts-library';

const result: number = addNumbers(5, 3); // TypeScript provides type information

7. Versioning and Maintenance

When maintaining a custom TypeScript library, it's essential to follow semantic versioning (semver) practices. Update your library's version number appropriately when making changes to ensure users can safely update their dependencies.

Additionally, consider adding documentation, tests, and continuous integration to enhance the quality and usability of your library.

Building custom TypeScript libraries empowers you to create reusable, type-safe code that can benefit both your projects and the broader developer community. By following best practices and making your library available through npm, you can contribute to a more robust TypeScript ecosystem.

6.5 Best Practices for Framework Integration

Integrating TypeScript with popular JavaScript frameworks is a common practice to build robust and type-safe web applications. In this section, we will explore best practices for integrating TypeScript with front-end frameworks like React, Angular, and Vue.js.

1. TypeScript Configuration

a. tsconfig.json

Ensure your tsconfig.json file is properly configured for your chosen framework. Each framework may have specific TypeScript requirements, so refer to their documentation for guidance. For example, when working with React, make sure to include "jsx": "react" in your tsconfig.json to enable JSX support.

b. Strict Mode

Consider enabling TypeScript's strict mode ("strict": true in tsconfig.json). Strict mode enforces stricter type checking, which can catch potential issues early in the development process.

2. Type Definitions

Frameworks often provide their own type definitions to enhance type safety. Always install and use these type definitions when available. For example, for React, you can install @types/react and @types/react-dom to get proper type checking and IntelliSense.

npm install @types/react @types/react-dom—save-dev

3. Use Functional Components (React)

In React, prefer functional components over class components. Functional components are easier to type and read, and they align well with TypeScript's type inference.

// Functional Component

import React from 'react';

interface Props {

message: string;

}

const MyComponent: React.FC<Props> = ({ message }) => {

```
return <div>{message}</div>;

};
```

4. Type Safety for Props (React)

When passing props to components, utilize TypeScript's generics to define prop types. This ensures type safety and provides clear documentation for component usage.

```
interface MyComponentProps {

message: string;

}

const MyComponent: React.FC<MyComponentProps> = ({ message }) => {

return <div>{message}</div>;

};
```

5. State Management (React)

If using state management libraries like Redux or Mobx, consider installing corresponding type definitions (e.g., @types/redux, @types/mobx) to benefit from type checking and auto-completion.

6. Angular Best Practices

When working with Angular, follow Angular's official documentation for TypeScript integration. Ensure your Angular project uses TypeScript for its configuration.

7. Vue.js Best Practices

For Vue.js, you can enhance type safety by using Vue's official TypeScript support. Install the vue and @vue/cli packages with TypeScript support to create Vue projects with TypeScript.

npm install -g @vue/cli

vue create my-project

Choose the TypeScript preset when creating a Vue.js project to enable TypeScript.

8. Third-party Libraries

When using third-party libraries and components, make sure to install their type definitions if available. Many popular libraries have type definitions on DefinitelyTyped, which can enhance type safety and developer experience.

9. Continuous Testing

Set up continuous integration (CI) and automated testing to catch type-related issues early in your development pipeline. Tools like Jest and Cypress can be configured to work seamlessly with TypeScript.

10. Documentation

Maintain clear and up-to-date documentation for your TypeScript integration practices within your team or project. Document any framework-specific TypeScript quirks and best practices for future reference.

Integrating TypeScript with front-end frameworks can significantly improve code quality and maintainability. By following these best practices, you can harness the full power of TypeScript while working with popular JavaScript frameworks, resulting in more reliable and maintainable applications.

Chapter 7: TypeScript in Backend Development

7.1 Setting Up a TypeScript Node.js Project

In this section, we will explore how to set up a TypeScript project for Node.js, enabling you to leverage TypeScript's benefits in backend development. TypeScript offers strong type checking, enhanced tooling, and modern JavaScript features, making it a valuable choice for server-side development.

1. Initializing a TypeScript Project

To start a new TypeScript Node.js project, you can use npm or yarn to initialize a new project directory. Here's how you can set up a basic project structure:

```
# Create a new directory for your Node.js project

mkdir my-ts-backend

cd my-ts-backend

# Initialize a new Node.js project with npm or yarn

npm init -y

# OR

yarn init -y
```

This will create a package.json file with default settings for your project.

2. Installing TypeScript

Next, you'll need to install TypeScript as a development dependency. Run the following command to install TypeScript:

npm install typescript—save-dev

 # OR

yarn add typescript—dev

3. Creating a TypeScript Configuration File

To configure TypeScript for your Node.js project, you'll need to create a tsconfig.json file. You can generate one using the TypeScript CLI:

npx tsc—init

The generated tsconfig.json file contains various configuration options that you can customize to match your project requirements. Make sure to set the "target" option to "ES6" or later to take advantage of modern JavaScript features.

4. Writing TypeScript Code

Now, you can start writing TypeScript code for your Node.js application. Create a TypeScript file (e.g., app.ts) and begin building your server-side logic. Here's a simple example of a Node.js server using the Express.js framework:

// Import required modules

import express **from** 'express';

// Create an Express application

```
const app = express();

const port = 3000;

// Define a route

app.get('/', (req, res) => {

res.send('Hello, TypeScript in Node.js!');

});

// Start the server

app.listen(port, () => {

console.log(`Server is running on port ${port}`);

});
```

5. Building and Running the Project

To compile your TypeScript code into JavaScript, run the TypeScript compiler (tsc) in your project directory:

```
npx tsc
```

This will generate JavaScript files in an out directory by default, according to your tsconfig.json settings.

To run your Node.js application, use the following command:

```
node out/app.js
```

Replace app.js with the name of your compiled TypeScript file.

6. Using Third-party Libraries

Node.js has a rich ecosystem of third-party libraries and modules. You can install and use them in your TypeScript project just like in regular JavaScript projects. Be sure to install type definitions for libraries that provide TypeScript support to benefit from type checking and IntelliSense.

npm install express @types/express—save

 # OR

yarn add express @types/express

7. Debugging

Visual Studio Code and other code editors provide excellent TypeScript debugging support for Node.js applications. You can set breakpoints, inspect variables, and step through your code to identify and fix issues.

8. Testing

Consider incorporating testing frameworks like Mocha, Jest, or Jasmine into your project for automated testing of your backend code. TypeScript seamlessly integrates with these testing frameworks, allowing you to write type-safe tests.

9. Continuous Integration

Set up continuous integration (CI) pipelines to automatically build and test your TypeScript Node.js application whenever changes are pushed to your version control system. Services like Travis CI, GitHub Actions, or Jenkins can be configured to work with TypeScript projects.

Setting up a TypeScript project for Node.js backend development provides the advantages of type safety, modern JavaScript features, and enhanced tooling. By following the steps in this section, you can create robust and maintainable server-side applications with TypeScript.

7.2 TypeScript with Express.js and Other Back-end Frameworks

When developing a Node.js backend with TypeScript, one common choice is to use a web framework like Express.js. In this section, we'll explore how to set up a TypeScript project with Express.js and discuss some best practices for developing type-safe APIs. Keep in mind that the concepts discussed here can be applied to other Node.js backend frameworks as well.

1. Installing Express.js and Required Dependencies

Start by creating a new TypeScript project or use an existing one, as described in the previous section. Next, you'll need to install Express.js and any additional dependencies you may require. Here's how to install Express.js and TypeScript declarations for it:

```
npm install express @types/express—save

# OR

yarn add express @types/express
```

2. Creating an Express App

Now, let's create a simple Express.js app in TypeScript. Create a TypeScript file (e.g., app.ts) and set up your Express application:

```
import express, { Request, Response } from 'express';
```

```
const app = express();

const port = 3000;

app.get('/', (req: Request, res: Response) => {

res.send('Hello, Express.js with TypeScript!');

});

app.listen(port, () => {

console.log(`Server is running on port ${port}`);

});
```

In the code above, we import express, Request, and Response types from the Express.js and TypeScript declaration files. This allows TypeScript to perform type checking on the request and response objects.

3. Defining API Routes

When building APIs, it's important to define routes and controllers. Here's an example of creating a simple API route with TypeScript:

```
interface User {

id: number;

username: string;

}

const users: User[] = [

{ id: 1, username: 'user1' },

{ id: 2, username: 'user2' },
```

```
];

app.get('/users', (req: Request, res: Response) => {

res.json(users);

});
```

In this example, we define an interface User to represent the shape of a user object. The /users route returns a JSON response containing an array of user objects.

4. Middleware and Error Handling

Middleware functions play a crucial role in Express.js applications. TypeScript allows you to define custom middleware with type checking. For instance, you can create middleware to handle authentication, authorization, or request validation, and ensure that the expected data types are used.

```
function authenticate(req: Request, res: Response, next: Function) {

// Implement authentication logic

if (req.headers.authorization !== 'Bearer myAuthToken') {

res.status(401).send('Unauthorized');

} else {

next();

}

}

app.use(authenticate);
```

// Add other routes and middleware as needed

5. Type-safe Request Body and Query Parameters

To ensure type safety when handling request body and query parameters, you can use TypeScript interfaces. Here's an example of defining an interface for request data:

```
interface CreateUserRequest {

username: string;

email: string;

}

app.post('/users', (req: Request<{}, {}, CreateUserRequest>, res: Response) => {

const { username, email } = req.body;

// Validate and create the user

// ...

});
```

By specifying the CreateUserRequest type for the request body, TypeScript provides type checking for the req.body object.

6. Database Integration

When working with databases, consider using an Object-Relational Mapping (ORM) library like TypeORM or Sequelize. These libraries have TypeScript support and can help you maintain type safety when interacting with the database.

7. Testing

Use testing frameworks like Mocha, Jest, or Supertest for unit testing and integration testing of your Express.js routes and middleware. TypeScript can be seamlessly integrated with these testing frameworks to provide type-safe testing.

8. Documentation

Consider using tools like Swagger or OpenAPI to generate API documentation. You can use TypeScript's type annotations to ensure that your API documentation remains consistent with your actual code.

In summary, using TypeScript with Express.js and other backend frameworks in Node.js allows you to build type-safe and maintainable APIs. By leveraging TypeScript's strong typing capabilities and following best practices, you can catch errors early in the development process and create robust backend applications.

7.3 Managing Database Interactions with TypeScript

In backend development, managing database interactions is a crucial aspect of building web applications. Whether you're using relational databases like PostgreSQL or MySQL, NoSQL databases like MongoDB, or other data stores, TypeScript can help ensure type safety and maintainability when working with databases.

1. Connecting to a Database

When connecting to a database, you'll typically use a database driver or Object-Relational Mapping (ORM) library. Many popular databases have TypeScript-compatible libraries and type definitions available. Here's an example of connecting to a PostgreSQL database using the pg library and TypeScript:

```typescript
import { Pool } from 'pg';

// Create a PostgreSQL database pool

const pool = new Pool({

user: 'your_user',

host: 'localhost',

database: 'your_database',

password: 'your_password',

port: 5432, // PostgreSQL default port

});

// Test the database connection

pool.query('SELECT NOW()', (err, res) => {

if (err) {

console.error('Error connecting to PostgreSQL:', err);

} else {

console.log('Connected to PostgreSQL');

}

});
```

In this example, we import the Pool class from the pg library to create a connection pool to a PostgreSQL database. Make sure to replace the connection details with your own.

2. Type-safe Models

To ensure type safety when working with database models, you can define TypeScript interfaces or classes that represent the structure of your data. For example, if you have a User table in your database, you can define a TypeScript interface like this:

interface User {

id: number;

username: string;

email: string;

created_at: Date;

}

This interface defines the expected structure of a user object, including the data types of each field.

3. Using an ORM

Using an Object-Relational Mapping (ORM) library like TypeORM, Sequelize, or Prisma can simplify database interactions in TypeScript projects. ORMs provide a way to define models, relationships, and queries in TypeScript code, which is then translated into SQL or NoSQL queries.

Here's an example of defining a User model using TypeORM:

```typescript
import { Entity, PrimaryGeneratedColumn, Column } from 'typeorm';

@Entity()

class User {

@PrimaryGeneratedColumn()

id: number;

@Column()

username: string;

@Column()

email: string;

@Column({ type: 'timestamp', default: () => 'CURRENT_TIMESTAMP' })

created_at: Date;

}
```

In this code, we use decorators provided by TypeORM to define the User entity and its properties. TypeORM will automatically generate database schema and queries based on this TypeScript code.

4. Performing Database Operations

With your database connection and models in place, you can perform database operations such as inserts, updates, selects, and deletes. TypeScript's type checking ensures that you're working with the correct data types.

```typescript
const newUser: User = {
```

```
  username: 'john_doe',

  email: 'john@example.com',

};
```

// Insert a new user

```
const insertedUser: User = await userRepository.save(newUser);
```

// Find a user by username

```
const foundUser: User | undefined = await userRepository.findOne({ username: 'john_doe' });
```

// Update a user's email

```
foundUser.email = 'new_email@example.com';

await userRepository.save(foundUser);
```

In this example, we use TypeORM to insert a new user, find a user by username, and update a user's email address.

5. Error Handling and Transactions

When working with databases, error handling and transaction management are critical. TypeScript allows you to define custom error types and handle database-related errors gracefully. Additionally, you can use transactions to ensure the consistency of database operations.

```
try {

await getManager().transaction(async (transactionalEntityManager) => {

const user1 = new User();
```

```
user1.username = 'user1';

user1.email = 'user1@example.com';

const user2 = new User();

user2.username = 'user2';

user2.email = 'user2@example.com';

await transactionalEntityManager.save(User, user1);

await transactionalEntityManager.save(User, user2);

// If an error occurs, the entire transaction will be rolled back

if (someCondition) {

throw new Error('Custom error');

}

});

} catch (error) {

console.error('Database error:', error);

}
```

6. Database Migrations

When your database schema evolves, you may need to perform
database migrations to update the schema without losing existing
data. Many ORM libraries, including TypeORM, provide tools for
managing database migrations in TypeScript projects.

7. Testing Database Code

To ensure the reliability of your database-related code, write unit tests and integration tests. Libraries like Jest and TypeORM provide testing utilities for TypeScript projects. Mocking database connections and using an in-memory database during testing can help isolate your tests.

In summary, TypeScript's strong typing and tooling support make it a powerful choice for managing database interactions in backend development. Whether you're using a traditional SQL database or a NoSQL data store, TypeScript helps you maintain type safety, catch errors early, and build robust backend applications.

7.4 Building RESTful APIs in TypeScript

Creating RESTful APIs is a common task in backend development, and TypeScript can greatly enhance the development process by providing strong typing and error checking. In this section, we'll explore how to build RESTful APIs in TypeScript, focusing on Express.js, one of the most popular Node.js frameworks.

1. Setting Up the Project

Before building your RESTful API, you need to set up your TypeScript project. You can use tools like tsc (TypeScript Compiler) and npm or yarn to manage dependencies and build your project. Ensure that you have TypeScript and Node.js installed.

npm init -y

npm install express @types/express typescript ts-node

Create a tsconfig.json file to configure TypeScript:

```
{

"compilerOptions": {

"target": "ES6",

"module": "CommonJS",

"outDir": "./dist",

"rootDir": "./src",

"strict": true,

"esModuleInterop": true

},

"include": ["src/**/*.ts"],

"exclude": ["node_modules"]

}
```

Create a src folder in your project directory to store your TypeScript source files.

2. Creating an Express.js Server

Next, create an Express.js server in TypeScript. Create an app.ts file in the src directory:

```
import express, { Request, Response } from 'express';

const app = express();

const port = process.env.PORT || 3000;

app.use(express.json());
```

```
app.get('/', (req: Request, res: Response) => {

res.send('Hello, World!');

});

app.listen(port, () => {

console.log(`Server is running on port ${port}`);

});
```

In this code, we import the necessary modules and set up a basic Express.js server with a single route that responds with "Hello, World!" when accessed via a GET request.

3. Creating API Endpoints

To create RESTful API endpoints, define routes and handlers for different HTTP methods (GET, POST, PUT, DELETE, etc.). Here's an example of creating a simple CRUD (Create, Read, Update, Delete) API for a list of items:

```
interface Item {

id: number;

name: string;

}

let items: Item[] = [

{ id: 1, name: 'Item 1' },

{ id: 2, name: 'Item 2' },

];
```

```typescript
// Get all items

app.get('/api/items', (req: Request, res: Response) => {

res.json(items);

});

// Get a single item by ID

app.get('/api/items/:id', (req: Request, res: Response) => {

const itemId = parseInt(req.params.id);

const item = items.find((i) => i.id === itemId);

if (item) {

res.json(item);

} else {

res.status(404).json({ error: 'Item not found' });

}

});

// Create a new item

app.post('/api/items', (req: Request, res: Response) => {

const newItem: Item = req.body;

newItem.id = Math.max(...items.map((i) => i.id), 0) + 1;

items.push(newItem);

res.status(201).json(newItem);
```

```
});

// Update an existing item

app.put('/api/items/:id', (req: Request, res: Response) => {

const itemId = parseInt(req.params.id);

const updatedItem: Item = req.body;

const index = items.findIndex((i) => i.id === itemId);

if (index !== -1) {

items[index] = { ...items[index], ...updatedItem };

res.json(items[index]);

} else {

res.status(404).json({ error: 'Item not found' });

}

});

// Delete an item by ID

app.delete('/api/items/:id', (req: Request, res: Response) => {

const itemId = parseInt(req.params.id);

const index = items.findIndex((i) => i.id === itemId);

if (index !== -1) {

items.splice(index, 1);

res.status(204).send();
```

```
} else {

res.status(404).json({ error: 'Item not found' });

}

});
```

In this example, we define routes for listing all items, getting a single item by ID, creating a new item, updating an existing item, and deleting an item by ID. The routes use TypeScript's strong typing to ensure that the request and response objects adhere to the expected data structures.

4. Middleware and Validation

You can use middleware functions to perform request validation, authentication, and authorization. Middleware functions can be applied globally to all routes or selectively to specific routes.

Here's an example of middleware for validating request data:

```
function validateItem(req: Request, res: Response, next: Function) {

const newItem: Item = req.body;

if (!newItem || !newItem.name) {

res.status(400).
```

7.5 Performance Considerations in TypeScript Backend Development

When building backend applications with TypeScript, performance is a critical consideration. A well-performing backend can handle high traffic, reduce response times, and ensure a smooth user experience. In this section, we'll explore various performance considerations and optimization techniques for TypeScript backend development.

1. Optimize Database Queries

Efficiently querying the database is often a bottleneck in backend performance. To optimize database queries:

- Use indexing for columns frequently used in WHERE clauses.

- Employ database query caching to reduce redundant queries.

- Consider denormalization for frequently accessed data.

- Utilize database connection pooling to manage connections efficiently.

Here's an example of using a connection pool with PostgreSQL using the pg library:

```typescript
import { Pool } from 'pg';

const pool = new Pool({

user: 'your_user',

host: 'your_host',

database: 'your_db',

password: 'your_password',

port: 5432,
```

```javascript
});

// Use the pool to query the database

pool.query('SELECT * FROM users', (err, res) => {

if (err) {

console.error('Error executing query', err);

} else {

console.log('Query result:', res.rows);

}

});
```

2. Caching

Caching frequently accessed data can significantly improve response times. Consider using in-memory caches like Redis or Memcached to store data that doesn't change frequently.

```javascript
import redis from 'redis';

const client = redis.createClient();

// Cache a value for 10 minutes

const key = 'myData';

const data = { foo: 'bar' };

client.setex(key, 600, JSON.stringify(data));

// Retrieve data from cache

client.get(key, (err, reply) => {
```

```javascript
if (err) {

console.error('Error retrieving data from cache', err);

} else {

const cachedData = JSON.parse(reply);

console.log('Cached data:', cachedData);

}

});
```

3. Compression and Content Delivery

Compressing responses and leveraging Content Delivery Networks (CDNs) can reduce the load on your server and improve frontend performance. Use middleware like compression to enable gzip or brotli compression in your Express.js application.

```javascript
import express from 'express';

import compression from 'compression';

const app = express();

// Use compression middleware

app.use(compression());

// ... Define your routes and handlers
```

4. Load Balancing

If your application experiences high traffic, distribute the load across multiple servers using load balancing techniques. Tools like Nginx or dedicated load balancer services can help achieve this.

5. Profiling and Monitoring

Regularly profile your application to identify performance bottlenecks. Tools like Node.js's built-in profiler and external services like New Relic or Datadog can provide insights into your application's performance.

6. Caching at the Application Level

Consider caching at the application level to store frequently used data or results of complex calculations. Libraries like node-cache can help with in-memory caching within your Node.js application.

```typescript
import NodeCache from 'node-cache';

const cache = new NodeCache();

// Store data in the cache

const key = 'myData';

const data = { foo: 'bar' };

cache.set(key, data, 3600); // Cache for 1 hour

// Retrieve data from the cache

const cachedData = cache.get(key);

if (cachedData) {

console.log('Cached data:', cachedData);

}
```

7. Optimizing Dependencies

Audit and optimize your project's dependencies. Remove unnecessary packages and ensure that you're using the latest versions to benefit from performance improvements and security fixes.

8. Use Asynchronous Code

Leverage asynchronous programming to handle concurrent requests efficiently. Use asynchronous libraries and patterns to prevent blocking operations that can slow down your server.

```
app.get('/api/resource', async (req, res) => {

try {

const data = await fetchDataFromDatabase();

res.json(data);

} catch (error) {

console.error('Error fetching data', error);

res.status(500).json({ error: 'Internal server error' });

}

});
```

9. Load Testing

Perform load testing on your backend to simulate heavy traffic and identify performance limitations. Tools like Apache JMeter or artillery.io can help you assess how your application handles high loads.

10. Vertical and Horizontal Scaling

Consider vertical scaling (adding more resources to a single server) and horizontal scaling (adding more servers) to handle increased traffic. Containerization and orchestration tools like Docker and Kubernetes simplify scaling strategies.

11. Continual Monitoring and Optimization

Regularly monitor your application's performance in production and implement ongoing optimizations. Performance tuning is an iterative process that evolves with your application's growth and usage patterns.

By addressing these performance considerations and implementing optimization techniques, you can ensure that your TypeScript backend applications are responsive and capable of handling real-world workloads effectively.

Chapter 8: Testing and Quality Assurance

8.1 Writing Unit Tests in TypeScript

Unit testing is an essential practice in software development to ensure that individual units of code function as expected. In TypeScript, unit testing can be accomplished using various testing frameworks such as Jest, Mocha, and Jasmine. In this section, we'll focus on writing unit tests using Jest, a popular testing framework for TypeScript.

Setting Up Jest

Before writing unit tests, you need to set up Jest in your TypeScript project. Jest provides a test runner, assertion library, and mocking capabilities.

1. Install Jest and the required dependencies as development dependencies:

npm install—save-dev jest @types/jest ts-jest

1. Configure Jest by creating a jest.config.js file in your project root:

module.exports = {

preset: 'ts-jest',

testEnvironment: 'node',

roots: ['<rootDir>/src'],

```
testMatch: ['**/*.test.ts'],

moduleFileExtensions: ['ts', 'tsx', 'js', 'jsx', 'json', 'node'],

};
```

This configuration sets up Jest to work with TypeScript files (.ts) and looks for test files with a .test.ts extension in the src directory.

Writing Unit Tests

Let's assume you have a simple TypeScript function that you want to test:

```
// src/math.ts

export function add(a: number, b: number): number {

return a + b;

}
```

To write a unit test for this function, create a test file with the same name as the source file and append .test.ts to it:

```
// src/math.test.ts

import { add } from './math';

test('adds two numbers', () => {

expect(add(1, 2)).toBe(3);

expect(add(-1, 1)).toBe(0);

expect(add(0, 0)).toBe(0);

});
```

In this example, we import the add function from math.ts and use Jest's test function to define test cases. We use the expect function to make assertions about the function's behavior.

Running Tests

You can run your tests using the jest command:

npx jest

Jest will discover and execute all test files in your project based on the configuration in jest.config.js. It will display the test results in the terminal.

Mocking Dependencies

When testing functions that depend on external services or modules, you may want to mock those dependencies to isolate the unit you're testing. Jest provides powerful mocking capabilities to achieve this.

```typescript
import { fetchData } from './dataService';

jest.mock('./dataService'); // Mock the entire module

test('fetchData returns mock data', async () => {

const mockData = { id: 1, name: 'John Doe' };

(fetchData as jest.Mock).mockResolvedValue(mockData);

const result = await fetchData();

expect(result).toEqual(mockData);

});
```

In this example, we mock the dataService module and specify the behavior of the fetchData function using mockResolvedValue. This allows us to control the response of the dependency during testing.

Conclusion

Unit testing in TypeScript with Jest is a powerful way to ensure the correctness of your code. By following best practices for writing tests and leveraging Jest's features, you can build robust and maintainable software with confidence in its quality.

8.2 Integration Testing Strategies

Integration testing is a crucial aspect of quality assurance in software development. Unlike unit testing, which focuses on testing individual components or units of code in isolation, integration testing verifies the interaction between different components, modules, or services within an application. In this section, we will explore various integration testing strategies and how TypeScript can be used to implement them effectively.

The Importance of Integration Testing

Integration testing is essential for several reasons:

1. **Detecting Integration Issues:** Integration tests help uncover issues that may arise when multiple components interact, such as data inconsistencies, communication problems, or unexpected behavior due to interactions.
2. **Realistic Scenarios:** Integration tests simulate real-world scenarios where various parts of the system work together, providing confidence in the application's behavior under actual conditions.
3. **End-to-End Verification:** Integration tests can cover end-

to-end workflows, ensuring that the entire system functions correctly from the user's perspective.

Types of Integration Testing

Integration testing can take various forms, depending on the scope and complexity of the application:

1. **Component Integration Testing:** Focuses on testing the interactions between individual components or modules within the application.
2. **API Integration Testing:** Tests the integration of an application's APIs or services with external APIs, databases, or microservices.
3. **UI Integration Testing:** Ensures that the user interface (UI) components interact correctly with the backend services and APIs.

Implementing Integration Tests in TypeScript

To implement integration tests in TypeScript, you can leverage testing frameworks and libraries like Jest, Supertest, and Axios. Here's a basic outline of the process:

1. **Setup:** Create a separate test suite for integration tests, and configure any necessary test environment settings.
2. **Test Database:** If your application uses a database, you may need to set up a test database or use an in-memory database during testing.
3. **Test Client:** Use libraries like Supertest or Axios to simulate HTTP requests to your application's endpoints or APIs.
4. **Assertions:** Make assertions about the responses and behavior of your application based on the integration

scenarios you want to test.

Example Integration Test (Using Jest and Supertest)

Let's consider a simple example where we want to test an API endpoint for creating a new user. We'll use Jest and Supertest to implement the integration test:

```javascript
import supertest from 'supertest';

import app from './app'; // Import your Express application

const request = supertest(app);

describe('User API Integration Tests', () => {

it('should create a new user', async () => {

const newUser = { username: 'john_doe', email: 'john@example.com' };

// Send a POST request to create a new user

const response = await request.post('/api/users').send(newUser);

// Assertions

expect(response.status).toBe(201);

expect(response.body).toHaveProperty('id');

expect(response.body.username).toBe(newUser.username);

expect(response.body.email).toBe(newUser.email);

});

});
```

In this example, we use Supertest to send a POST request to the /api/users endpoint of our Express application and make assertions about the response.

Test Isolation and Cleanup

To ensure test isolation, it's essential to clean up any data or state created during integration tests to prevent interference between different tests. Consider using tools like Jest's beforeAll and afterAll hooks or database transactions to achieve proper test isolation.

Conclusion

Integration testing is a critical part of the software development process, helping to identify and resolve issues that may arise when different parts of an application interact. By using TypeScript in combination with testing frameworks and libraries, you can implement effective integration tests that provide confidence in your application's functionality and reliability.

8.3 End-to-End Testing in a TypeScript Environment

End-to-end (E2E) testing is a critical phase in software testing where the entire application is tested as a whole to ensure that all components and interactions work correctly. E2E tests simulate user interactions and verify that the application functions as expected from the user's perspective. In this section, we'll explore E2E testing strategies in a TypeScript environment and discuss tools and libraries that can be used to implement them.

Importance of End-to-End Testing

E2E testing is essential for several reasons:

1. **User-Centric Testing:** E2E tests focus on the user's experience, ensuring that the application performs as intended from the user's perspective.
2. **Complex Workflow Verification:** E2E tests cover complex user workflows that involve multiple components, services, and interactions.
3. **Realistic Scenarios:** E2E tests mimic real-world scenarios, helping identify issues that may arise in production.

Implementing E2E Tests in TypeScript

To implement E2E tests in a TypeScript environment, you can use testing frameworks and libraries like Cypress, Playwright, or Puppeteer. These tools provide features for automating browser interactions and validating application behavior. Here's a basic outline of the process:

1. **Setup:** Set up your E2E testing environment by installing the necessary tools and configuring your testing framework.
2. **Write Test Scenarios:** Define E2E test scenarios that cover different user journeys through your application.
3. **Automate Interactions:** Use the testing tool to automate user interactions, such as clicking buttons, filling out forms, and navigating between pages.
4. **Assertions:** Define assertions to verify that the application behaves correctly at various stages of the test scenarios.
5. **Run Tests:** Execute the E2E tests, and collect test results and logs for analysis.

Example E2E Test (Using Cypress)

Let's consider an example E2E test using Cypress for a simple web application. We'll write a test that navigates to a login page, enters valid credentials, and verifies that the user is logged in successfully.

```ts
// cypress/integration/login.spec.ts

describe('Login Page E2E Test', () => {

it('should log in with valid credentials', () => {

// Visit the login page

cy.visit('/login');

// Enter valid credentials and submit the form

cy.get('input[name="username"]').type('john_doe');

cy.get('input[name="password"]').type('password123');

cy.get('button[type="submit"]').click();

// Verify that the user is logged in

cy.url().should('eq', 'https://example.com/dashboard');

cy.get('h1').should('contain.text', 'Welcome, John Doe!');

});

});
```

In this Cypress test, we visit the login page, interact with the login form, and make assertions about the application's behavior.

Test Isolation and Cleanup

E2E tests can be resource-intensive and time-consuming. Proper test isolation and cleanup are crucial to ensure that tests run consistently and do not interfere with each other. Tools like Cypress provide mechanisms for setting up and tearing down test data and state.

Continuous Integration (CI) Integration

E2E tests are often integrated into continuous integration (CI) pipelines to ensure that the application remains functional across different environments and configurations. CI/CD tools like Jenkins, Travis CI, or GitHub Actions can be configured to run E2E tests automatically.

Conclusion

End-to-end testing in a TypeScript environment is a valuable practice for validating that your application functions correctly from a user's perspective. By using testing frameworks and libraries, you can automate user interactions, define test scenarios, and ensure that your application behaves as expected in various situations. E2E testing complements unit and integration testing to provide comprehensive test coverage for your application.

8.4 Code Quality Tools for TypeScript

Maintaining code quality is crucial in any software development project. Poorly maintained code can lead to bugs, reduce maintainability, and hinder collaboration among team members. In this section, we'll explore code quality tools and practices for TypeScript that can help you ensure the robustness and readability of your codebase.

TypeScript Linter: TSLint and ESLint

Linters are tools that analyze your code for potential issues, coding style violations, and adherence to coding standards. In the TypeScript ecosystem, two popular linters are TSLint and ESLint.

- **TSLint (Deprecated):** TSLint was the original TypeScript linter but has been deprecated in favor of ESLint. If you're working with an older codebase that uses TSLint, consider migrating to ESLint.

- **ESLint with TypeScript:** ESLint has extensive TypeScript support through plugins and configurations. You can configure ESLint to enforce coding standards, catch common errors, and maintain consistent code style in your TypeScript projects.

Installing ESLint with TypeScript:

 # Install ESLint and TypeScript ESLint plugin

npm install eslint @typescript-eslint/eslint-plugin @typescript-eslint/parser—save-dev

Configuring ESLint for TypeScript:

Create an .eslintrc.js or .eslintrc.json configuration file in your project and specify your ESLint rules, TypeScript parser, and plugins.

// .eslintrc.js

module.exports = {

parser: '@typescript-eslint/parser',

```
plugins: ['@typescript-eslint'],

extends: ['eslint:recommended', 'plugin:@typescript-eslint/
recommended'],

rules: {

// Define your custom ESLint rules here

},

};
```

Code Formatter: Prettier

Prettier is an opinionated code formatter that enforces consistent code style across your project. It automatically formats your code to adhere to a predefined set of rules, eliminating debates about code style.

Installing Prettier:

```
# Install Prettier and Prettier plugin for ESLint

npm install prettier eslint-config-prettier
eslint-plugin-prettier—save-dev
```

Configuring Prettier:

Create a .prettierrc.js or .prettierrc.json configuration file in your project to define your code formatting preferences.

```
// .prettierrc.js

module.exports = {

semi: true,
```

trailingComma: 'all',

singleQuote: **true**,

printWidth: 80,

// Define more formatting options as needed

};

You can integrate Prettier with ESLint using the ESLint Prettier plugin (eslint-config-prettier) to ensure that your ESLint rules and Prettier rules do not conflict.

Static Analysis: TypeScript Compiler

TypeScript itself acts as a static analysis tool that checks your code for type errors and provides type information to improve code quality. TypeScript's strict type checking can catch many bugs at compile time, leading to more reliable code.

To take full advantage of TypeScript's static analysis capabilities, configure your tsconfig.json file to use strict compiler options, such as enabling the strict flag.

*// **tsconfig.json***

{

"compilerOptions": {

"strict": **true**,

*// **Other compiler options***

}

}

Code Coverage: Istanbul and Jest

Code coverage tools like Istanbul and Jest can help you assess the percentage of your code that is covered by tests. These tools generate reports that highlight areas of your codebase that need more test coverage.

- **Istanbul:** Istanbul is a popular code coverage tool for JavaScript and TypeScript. It works well with various testing frameworks and can be integrated into your build process.

- **Jest:** If you're using Jest as your testing framework, it includes built-in code coverage reporting. Jest can generate coverage reports in different formats, making it easy to assess the quality of your tests.

Continuous Integration (CI) Integration

To maintain code quality consistently, integrate code quality tools like ESLint, Prettier, and code coverage analysis into your continuous integration (CI) pipeline. CI services like GitHub Actions, Travis CI, and Jenkins can be configured to run these tools automatically as part of your code review and deployment process.

By leveraging these code quality tools and practices in your TypeScript projects, you can ensure that your codebase remains clean, readable, and robust, contributing to smoother development workflows and more reliable software.

8.5 Continuous Integration and Deployment with TypeScript

Continuous Integration (CI) and Continuous Deployment (CD) are essential practices in modern software development. They help automate the building, testing, and deployment of your TypeScript applications, ensuring that your code remains reliable and up-to-date. In this section, we'll explore how to set up CI/CD pipelines for TypeScript projects.

CI/CD Tools and Services

Several CI/CD tools and services are widely used in the software industry. Some popular ones include:

- **GitHub Actions:** If you're using GitHub as your version control platform, GitHub Actions provides a seamless way to automate CI/CD workflows. You can define workflows in YAML files within your repository, specifying the steps to build, test, and deploy your TypeScript application.

- **Travis CI:** Travis CI is a popular CI/CD service that integrates with various version control systems. It allows you to define CI/CD pipelines in a .travis.yml configuration file. Travis CI supports TypeScript projects and can run tests and deploy your code to various platforms.

- **Jenkins:** Jenkins is an open-source automation server that offers extensive customization and flexibility. You can set up Jenkins to build, test, and deploy your TypeScript applications by defining pipelines using Jenkinsfile or other configuration methods.

- **CircleCI:** CircleCI is a cloud-based CI/CD platform that supports TypeScript projects. It allows you to define jobs and workflows in YAML configuration files, similar to other CI/CD tools.

Setting Up a Basic CI/CD Pipeline

To set up a basic CI/CD pipeline for your TypeScript project, follow these general steps:

1. **Version Control:** Ensure your TypeScript project is hosted on a version control platform like GitHub, GitLab, or Bitbucket.
2. **Choose a CI/CD Service:** Select a CI/CD service that suits your project's requirements and integrates well with your version control platform.
3. **Configuration File:** Create a configuration file (e.g., .github/workflows/main.yml for GitHub Actions, .travis.yml for Travis CI) in your repository to define your CI/CD workflow.
4. **Define Workflow Steps:** In the configuration file, specify the workflow steps, including building your TypeScript code, running tests, and deploying the application if all tests pass.
5. **Environment Variables:** Securely store any sensitive information or environment variables needed for your CI/CD process. Most CI/CD services allow you to store secrets securely.
6. **Trigger Events:** Configure when the CI/CD pipeline should run. Common triggers include pushes to specific branches, pull requests, or manual triggers.
7. **Testing and Deployment:** Use appropriate tools and scripts to run tests, generate code coverage reports, and

deploy your application to the desired environment (e.g., staging or production).

8. **Notifications:** Set up notifications and alerts to inform your team about the status of CI/CD runs. This helps quickly identify and address issues.

Example GitHub Actions Workflow

Here's a simplified example of a GitHub Actions workflow for a TypeScript project. This workflow builds and tests the project on each push to the main branch and deploys it to a staging environment if all tests pass.

 # .github/workflows/main.yml

name: CI/CD Pipeline

on:

push:

branches:

- main

jobs:

build:

runs-on: ubuntu-latest

steps:

- name: Checkout code

uses: actions/checkout@v2

- name: Install Node.js

```yaml
uses: actions/setup-node@v2

with:

node-version: '14'

- name: Install dependencies

run: npm install

- name: Build and test

run: npm run build && npm test

deploy:

needs: build

runs-on: ubuntu-latest

steps:

- name: Deploy to staging

run: |

if [ "${{ job.status }}" == "success" ]; then

# Add deployment script or commands here

fi
```

Keep in mind that this is a simplified example, and your actual CI/ CD pipeline may require additional steps or customizations based on your project's needs and infrastructure.

By implementing CI/CD for your TypeScript projects, you can streamline your development workflow, catch issues early, and ensure that your code is consistently deployed to production with minimal manual intervention.

Chapter 9: Advanced TypeScript Patterns

9.1 Design Patterns in TypeScript

Design patterns are proven solutions to common problems in software design. They provide a structured way to solve recurring issues and promote best practices. TypeScript, being a statically typed language, is well-suited for implementing design patterns. In this section, we'll explore some common design patterns and how they can be implemented in TypeScript.

Creational Patterns

Singleton Pattern

The Singleton pattern ensures that a class has only one instance and provides a global point of access to that instance. In TypeScript, you can implement it like this:

```typescript
class Singleton {

private static instance: Singleton;

private constructor() {}

static getInstance(): Singleton {

if (!Singleton.instance) {

Singleton.instance = new Singleton();

}

return Singleton.instance;
```

```
}

}
```

Factory Method Pattern

The Factory Method pattern defines an interface for creating an object but lets subclasses alter the type of objects that will be created. Here's an example:

```
interface Product {

operation(): string;

}

class ConcreteProductA implements Product {

operation(): string {

return 'Product A';

}

}

class ConcreteProductB implements Product {

operation(): string {

return 'Product B';

}

}

abstract class Creator {
```

```typescript
abstract factoryMethod(): Product;

someOperation(): string {

const product = this.factoryMethod();

return `Creator works with ${product.operation()}`;

}

}

class ConcreteCreatorA extends Creator {

factoryMethod(): Product {

return new ConcreteProductA();

}

}

class ConcreteCreatorB extends Creator {

factoryMethod(): Product {

return new ConcreteProductB();

}

}
```

Structural Patterns

Adapter Pattern

The Adapter pattern allows objects with incompatible interfaces to work together. TypeScript can make this pattern more convenient with its support for interfaces and classes. Here's a simplified example:

```typescript
interface Target {

request(): string;

}

class Adaptee {

specificRequest(): string {

return 'Adaptee request';

}

}

class Adapter implements Target {

private adaptee: Adaptee;

constructor(adaptee: Adaptee) {

this.adaptee = adaptee;

}

request(): string {

return `Adapter: ${this.adaptee.specificRequest()}`;

}

}
```

Composite Pattern

The Composite pattern lets you compose objects into tree structures to represent part-whole hierarchies. TypeScript's support for classes and inheritance makes it a natural fit for this pattern:

```typescript
abstract class Component {

abstract operation(): string;

}

class Leaf extends Component {

operation(): string {

return 'Leaf';

}

}

class Composite extends Component {

private children: Component[] = [];

add(component: Component): void {

this.children.push(component);

}

operation(): string {

const results: string[] = [];

for (const child of this.children) {

results.push(child.operation());
```

```typescript
  }

  return `Composite(${results.join(', ')})`;

  }

}
```

Behavioral Patterns

Observer Pattern

The Observer pattern defines a one-to-many relationship between objects. When one object changes state, all its dependents are notified and updated automatically. TypeScript's event system and classes make implementing this pattern straightforward:

```typescript
class Subject {

private observers: Observer[] = [];

addObserver(observer: Observer): void {

this.observers.push(observer);

}

removeObserver(observer: Observer): void {

this.observers = this.observers.filter((o) => o !== observer);

}

notifyObservers(): void {

for (const observer of this.observers) {

observer.update();
```

```typescript
  }
 }
}

class ConcreteSubject extends Subject {

private state: number = 0;

getState(): number {

return this.state;

}

setState(state: number): void {

this.state = state;

this.notifyObservers();

}

}

interface Observer {

update(): void;

}

class ConcreteObserver implements Observer {
private subject: ConcreteSubject;

constructor(subject: ConcreteSubject) {

this.subject = subject;
```

```typescript
this.subject.addObserver(this);

}

update(): void {

console.log(`Observer received update: ${this.subject.getState()}`);

}

}
```

These are just a few examples of design patterns that can be applied in TypeScript. By understanding and utilizing design patterns, you can write more maintainable and efficient code that follows established best practices. Design patterns are tools in the developer's toolbox, and choosing the right pattern for a specific problem can greatly improve the quality of your TypeScript applications.

9.2 Functional Programming Techniques

Functional programming is a programming paradigm that treats computation as the evaluation of mathematical functions and avoids changing state and mutable data. TypeScript supports functional programming techniques, allowing you to write more concise and expressive code. In this section, we'll explore some functional programming concepts and how to use them in TypeScript.

First-Class Functions

In functional programming, functions are treated as first-class citizens, which means they can be assigned to variables, passed as arguments to other functions, and returned from functions. TypeScript fully supports first-class functions:

```typescript
// Assigning a function to a variable
```

```typescript
const add = (a: number, b: number) => a + b;

// Passing a function as an argument

const calculate = (fn: (a: number, b: number) => number, a:
number, b: number) => fn(a, b);

// Returning a function from a function

const multiplyBy = (factor: number) => (num: number) => num *
factor;

const result = calculate(add, 2, 3); // 5

const double = multiplyBy(2);

const doubledResult = double(4); // 8
```

Higher-Order Functions

Higher-order functions are functions that take one or more functions as arguments or return a function as their result. TypeScript allows you to create higher-order functions easily:

```typescript
// A higher-order function that applies a function to each element of an
array

const map = <T, U>(array: T[], fn: (value: T) => U): U[] => {

const result: U[] = [];

for (const item of array) {

result.push(fn(item));

}

return result;
```

```
};
```

```
const numbers = [1, 2, 3, 4, 5];
```

```
const squared = map(numbers, (num) => num ** 2); // [1, 4, 9, 16, 25]
```

Immutable Data

Immutable data means that data, once created, cannot be changed. TypeScript's type system can help you enforce immutability:

```
// Using readonly properties to create immutable objects

type Point = { readonly x: number; readonly y: number };

const point: Point = { x: 1, y: 2 };

// point.x = 3; // Error: Cannot assign to 'x' because it is a read-only property.

// Creating a new object with modifications (immutability)

const updatedPoint = { ...point, x: 3 };
```

Pure Functions

Pure functions are functions that always produce the same output for the same input and have no side effects. TypeScript encourages writing pure functions, which are easier to reason about and test:

```
// Impure function with side effect

let counter = 0;

const increment = (value: number): number => {

counter++;
```

```typescript
  return value + 1;

};

// Pure function with no side effect

const pureIncrement = (value: number): number => value + 1;

const result1 = increment(1); // result1 = 2, counter = 1 (side effect)

const result2 = pureIncrement(1); // result2 = 2 (no side effect)
```

Function Composition

Function composition is the process of combining two or more functions to produce a new function. TypeScript allows you to compose functions easily:

```typescript
// Function composition

const compose = <T, U, V>(fn1: (x: T) => U, fn2: (y: U) => V) =>
(input: T): V => fn2(fn1(input));

const addOne = (x: number) => x + 1;

const double = (x: number) => x * 2;

const addOneAndDouble = compose(addOne, double);

const result = addOneAndDouble(3); // 8 (double(addOne(3)))
```

These are some of the functional programming techniques that you can apply in TypeScript to write cleaner and more maintainable code. By embracing functional programming concepts, you can improve the readability and testability of your code while reducing the likelihood of bugs related to mutable state and side effects.

9.3 Reactive Programming with TypeScript

Reactive programming is a programming paradigm that deals with asynchronous data streams and the propagation of changes. It's commonly used in modern web development, especially when dealing with user interfaces and real-time applications. TypeScript provides excellent support for reactive programming, and in this section, we'll explore some of the key concepts and libraries for reactive programming.

Observables and RxJS

At the heart of reactive programming in TypeScript is the concept of observables. Observables represent sequences of values that can be observed over time. The RxJS library is a powerful tool for working with observables in TypeScript. To get started with RxJS, you'll need to install it:

```
npm install rxjs
```

Here's a basic example of creating and subscribing to an observable using RxJS:

```typescript
import { Observable } from 'rxjs';

// Creating an observable
const observable = new Observable<number>((observer) => {

observer.next(1);

observer.next(2);

observer.next(3);

observer.complete();
```

```
});

// Subscribing to the observable

observable.subscribe({

next: (value) => console.log(value),

complete: () => console.log('Observable completed'),

});
```

In this example, we create an observable that emits three values (1, 2, and 3) and completes. The subscribe method allows us to define what should happen when values are emitted and when the observable completes.

Operators in RxJS

RxJS provides a wide range of operators that you can use to transform, filter, combine, and manipulate observables. These operators make it easier to work with complex asynchronous data flows. Here's an example of using the map operator to transform values emitted by an observable:

```
import { Observable } from 'rxjs';

import { map } from 'rxjs/operators';

const numbers = new Observable<number>((observer) => {

observer.next(1);

observer.next(2);

observer.next(3);

observer.complete();
```

```
});

numbers

.pipe(

map((value) => value * 2) // Use the map operator to double the values

)

.subscribe({

next: (value) => console.log(value),

complete: () => console.log('Observable completed'),

});
```

The pipe method allows us to chain multiple operators together to create a data processing pipeline for observables.

Subjects in RxJS

Subjects are another essential concept in reactive programming with RxJS. A subject is both an observable and an observer, making it a powerful tool for multicasting values to multiple subscribers. Here's a simple example:

```
import { Subject } from 'rxjs';

// Creating a subject

const subject = new Subject<number>();

// Subscribing to the subject (multiple subscribers)

subject.subscribe((value) => console.log(`Subscriber 1: ${value}`));

subject.subscribe((value) => console.log(`Subscriber 2: ${value}`));
```

```
// Emitting values from the subject

subject.next(1);

subject.next(2);

subject.complete();
```

In this example, we create a subject and subscribe to it with two different subscribers. When we emit values using subject.next(), both subscribers receive the values.

Reactive programming with observables, operators, and subjects can simplify complex asynchronous code and help manage state changes in your applications. RxJS is a versatile library that provides the tools you need to work with reactive data streams effectively.

9.4 TypeScript Decorators in Depth

In TypeScript, decorators are a powerful and flexible feature that allows you to add metadata, modify behavior, or transform classes, methods, and properties during declaration. Decorators use the @decorator syntax, and they are widely used in modern web development, especially with frameworks like Angular.

Class Decorators

Class decorators are applied to class declarations and can be used to modify or enhance the behavior of the class. They take the class constructor as their only parameter and can return a new constructor or modify the existing one. Here's an example of a simple class decorator:

```
function myClassDecorator(target: Function) {

console.log(`Class decorator called on: ${target.name}`);
```

```
}

@myClassDecorator

class MyClass {

constructor() {

console.log('MyClass constructor called');

}

}

const myInstance = new MyClass();
```

In this example, the myClassDecorator function is a class decorator that logs the name of the decorated class. When we apply the @myClassDecorator decorator to the MyClass class, it logs "Class decorator called on: MyClass" when the class is declared.

Method Decorators

Method decorators are used to modify or enhance the behavior of methods within a class. They take three parameters: the target (class or prototype), the method name, and a property descriptor. Here's an example:

```
function myMethodDecorator(target: any, methodName: string, descriptor: PropertyDescriptor) {

console.log(`Method decorator called on: ${target.constructor.name}.${methodName}`);

}

class MyClass {
```

```typescript
@myMethodDecorator

myMethod() {

console.log('My method called');

}

}

const myInstance = new MyClass();

myInstance.myMethod();
```

In this example, the myMethodDecorator is applied to the myMethod function within the MyClass class. It logs "Method decorator called on: MyClass.myMethod" when the method is declared.

Property Decorators

Property decorators are used to modify or enhance the behavior of class properties. They take two parameters: the target (class or prototype) and the property name. Here's an example:

```typescript
function myPropertyDecorator(target: any, propertyName: string)
{

console.log(`Property              decorator            called            on:
${target.constructor.name}.${propertyName}`);

}

class MyClass {

@myPropertyDecorator

myProperty: string = 'My Property';
```

```
}
```

const myInstance = **new** MyClass();

console.log(myInstance.myProperty);

In this example, the myPropertyDecorator is applied to the myProperty property within the MyClass class. It logs "Property decorator called on: MyClass.myProperty" when the property is declared.

Decorators are a powerful tool in TypeScript, and they are commonly used in libraries and frameworks to add functionality or metadata to classes and their members. Understanding decorators can be particularly valuable when working with modern web development frameworks like Angular, where decorators play a significant role in defining components, services, and more.

9.5 Advanced Asynchronous Patterns in TypeScript

Asynchronous programming is a crucial aspect of modern software development, allowing applications to perform tasks concurrently and efficiently. In TypeScript, you have various techniques and patterns to handle asynchronous operations, ensuring your code remains maintainable and readable. This section explores some advanced asynchronous patterns and best practices in TypeScript.

Promises and Async/Await

Promises and async/await are fundamental asynchronous patterns in TypeScript. Promises represent a value that might be available now, in the future, or never, while async/await provides a more readable and synchronous-like syntax for working with asynchronous code.

```typescript
function fetchData(): Promise<string> {

return new Promise((resolve, reject) => {

setTimeout(() => {

resolve('Data fetched successfully');

}, 1000);

});

}

async function getData() {

try {

const result = await fetchData();

console.log(result);

} catch (error) {

console.error(error);

}

}

getData();
```

In this example, the fetchData function returns a Promise that resolves after a timeout. The getData function uses async/await to wait for the Promise to resolve and handles errors with a try/catch block.

Thunks and Redux

Thunks are a common pattern used in combination with Redux for managing asynchronous actions. They are functions that encapsulate a piece of asynchronous logic and can be dispatched like regular actions.

```typescript
import { createStore, applyMiddleware } from 'redux';

import thunk from 'redux-thunk';

// Action creators

function fetchDataStart() {

return { type: 'FETCH_DATA_START' };

}

function fetchDataSuccess(data: string) {

return { type: 'FETCH_DATA_SUCCESS', payload: data };

}

function fetchDataError(error: string) {

return { type: 'FETCH_DATA_ERROR', payload: error };

}

// Thunk

function fetchData() {

return async (dispatch: any) => {

dispatch(fetchDataStart());
```

```
try {

const result = await fetchDataFromAPI();

dispatch(fetchDataSuccess(result));

} catch (error) {

dispatch(fetchDataError(error.message));

}

};

}

// Redux store setup

const initialState = { loading: false, data: null, error: null };

function dataReducer(state = initialState, action: any) {

switch (action.type) {

// Reducer logic here

}

}

const store = createStore(dataReducer, applyMiddleware(thunk));

store.dispatch(fetchData());
```

In this example, we define action creators for starting, successful, and error states. The fetchData thunk dispatches these actions while performing an asynchronous operation. Redux middleware like redux-thunk enables the use of thunks within Redux.

Observables and RxJS

Observables and RxJS provide a powerful way to work with asynchronous data streams. They are often used in applications that require complex event handling and data transformations over time.

```typescript
import { Observable, of, throwError } from 'rxjs';

import { catchError, map, switchMap } from 'rxjs/operators';

function fetchData(): Observable<string> {

return of('Data fetched successfully').pipe(

map((data) => {

if (Math.random() < 0.5) {

return data;

} else {

throw new Error('Error fetching data');

}

}),

catchError((error) => throwError(error))

);

}

fetchData()

.pipe(
```

```
switchMap((data) => fetchData()) // Simulate another async
operation based on the result

)

.subscribe(

(result) => console.log(result),

(error) => console.error(error)

);
```

In this example, we create an Observable with RxJS's of operator and then use various operators like map, catchError, and switchMap to manipulate and handle asynchronous data.

These are just a few advanced asynchronous patterns you can leverage in TypeScript. Depending on your project's requirements, you may choose one or more of these patterns to handle asynchronous operations effectively and maintain code readability.

Chapter 10: TypeScript for Scalable Projects

10.1 Organizing Large Codebases with TypeScript

Managing a large codebase is a challenging task in any software project. TypeScript, with its strong typing and module system, offers several techniques and best practices for organizing and maintaining large codebases effectively. In this section, we'll explore strategies for structuring your TypeScript projects to enhance scalability, maintainability, and collaboration among team members.

Directory Structure

A well-defined directory structure is the foundation of organizing large TypeScript projects. It helps developers find files quickly and understand the project's architecture. Here's a commonly used directory structure for TypeScript projects:

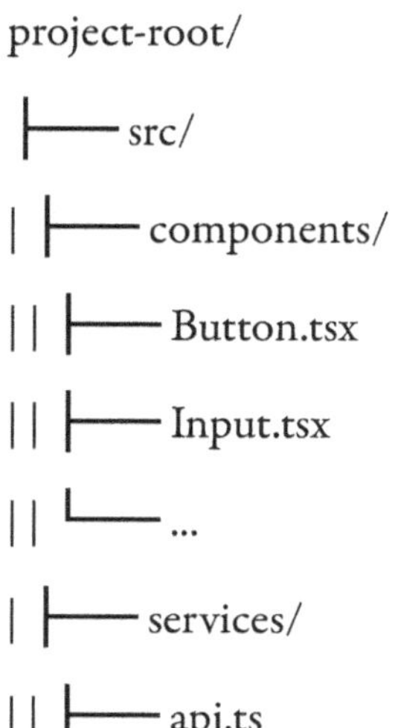

```
|   |   ├── authentication.ts
|   |   └── ...
|   ├── utils/
|   |   ├── helpers.ts
|   |   ├── constants.ts
|   |   └── ...
|   ├── pages/
|   |   ├── Home.tsx
|   |   ├── Dashboard.tsx
|   |   └── ...
|   ├── index.tsx
|   └── ...
├── tests/
|   ├── unit/
|   ├── integration/
|   └── ...
├── build/
├── node_modules/
├── package.json
├── tsconfig.json
```

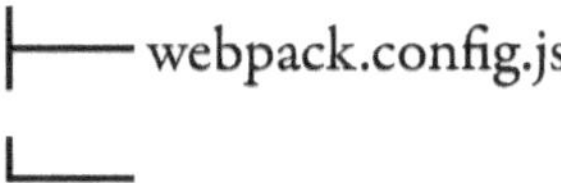

This structure separates different types of files into logical folders. The src/ folder contains your application's source code, while the tests/ directory holds your tests. A clear separation between components, services, utilities, and pages helps maintain order and readability.

Modules and Namespaces

TypeScript provides modules and namespaces to encapsulate code and prevent naming collisions. When dealing with a large codebase, consider using modules to organize related code into separate files. This makes it easier to manage dependencies and prevents global scope pollution.

```typescript
// Math.ts

export function add(a: number, b: number): number {

return a + b;

}

// Calculator.ts

import { add } from './Math';

export function multiply(a: number, b: number): number {

let result = 0;

for (let i = 0; i < a; i++) {

result = add(result, b);
```

```
}
```

return result;

```
}
```

In this example, the Math module exports a function, and the Calculator module imports and uses it. This modular approach simplifies code navigation and promotes reusability.

Dependency Management

Managing dependencies is crucial in large projects. Use a package manager like npm or yarn to track and install project dependencies. Create a package.json file to list your project's dependencies and devDependencies.

```json
{

"dependencies": {

"react": "^17.0.2",

"react-dom": "^17.0.2"

},

"devDependencies": {

"@types/react": "^17.0.31",

"@types/react-dom": "^17.0.10",

"typescript": "^4.5.4"

}

}
```

Using TypeScript's type definitions (@types) ensures type safety when working with third-party libraries.

Code Splitting

As your codebase grows, consider implementing code splitting techniques to reduce the initial bundle size and improve performance. Modern bundlers like Webpack and tools like dynamic import() enable you to split your code into smaller chunks that are loaded on-demand.

```
// Using dynamic import

const loadModule = async () => {

const module = await import('./module');

module.doSomething();

};

// Webpack code splitting configuration

module.exports = {

//...

optimization: {

splitChunks: {

chunks: 'all',

},

},

};
```

By dynamically importing modules and configuring your bundler to split chunks, you can optimize the loading of your application and enhance the user experience.

Documentation and Comments

Large codebases benefit from comprehensive documentation and meaningful comments. Document your functions, classes, and modules using tools like JSDoc. Clear comments help other developers understand your code's purpose and usage.

```
/**

* Adds two numbers.

* @param {number} a - The first number.

* @param {number} b - The second number.

* @returns {number} The sum of a and b.

*/

export function add(a: number, b: number): number {

return a + b;

}
```

Continuous Integration (CI) and Code Quality Tools

Implement CI pipelines to automate testing, code analysis, and code formatting. Tools like ESLint, Prettier, and TypeScript's tsc help maintain code quality and consistency.

```
# .github/workflows/ci.yml

name: CI
```

```yaml
on:
push:
branches:
- main
jobs:
build:
runs-on: ubuntu-latest
steps:
- name: Checkout code
uses: actions/checkout@v2
- name: Setup Node.js
uses: actions/setup-node@v2
with:
node-version: 14
- name: Install dependencies
run: npm install
- name: Run tests
run: npm test
- name: Check code formatting
run: npm run lint
```

By incorporating CI and code quality tools into your workflow, you can catch issues early and maintain code consistency.

In conclusion, organizing and maintaining large codebases with TypeScript requires careful planning and adherence to best practices. A well-structured directory layout, modular code, dependency management, code splitting, documentation, and CI pipelines are essential components of managing scalable TypeScript projects. These practices ensure your project remains maintainable and facilitates collaboration among team members, ultimately leading to a successful and sustainable software project.

10.2 Scalability Best Practices

Scalability is a critical aspect of large TypeScript projects. As your codebase grows, it's essential to follow best practices to ensure that your application remains maintainable, performant, and adaptable to future changes. In this section, we'll explore some key scalability best practices for TypeScript projects.

1. Modularity and Separation of Concerns

One of the fundamental principles of scalable software architecture is modularity. Divide your code into small, reusable, and self-contained modules. Each module should have a specific responsibility or concern. This approach makes it easier to reason about your code and allows for independent development and testing of modules.

// Example of a modular approach

// UserService.ts

export class UserService {

```
// Methods for user-related operations
}

// ProductService.ts

export class ProductService {

// Methods for product-related operations
}

// OrderService.ts

export class OrderService {

// Methods for order-related operations
}
```

2. Use Interfaces and Abstractions

Interfaces and abstractions provide clear contracts between different parts of your application. By defining interfaces for your components and services, you can ensure that they adhere to specific APIs. Abstractions like abstract classes or custom types can further enhance code quality and maintainability.

```
// Interface for a data repository

interface Repository<T> {

getById(id: number): T | undefined;

save(item: T): void;

// Other CRUD methods
}
```

```typescript
// Implementation of a UserRepository

class UserRepository implements Repository<User> {

// Implement the interface methods

}

// Usage of the UserRepository

const userRepository: Repository<User> = new UserRepository();
```

3. Dependency Injection

Dependency injection is a design pattern that promotes loose coupling between components. It allows you to inject dependencies (e.g., services) into other components instead of hardcoding them. TypeScript's strong typing system makes it easy to implement dependency injection.

```typescript
// Example of dependency injection

class OrderService {

constructor(private userService: UserService) {}

// Use the userService instance in methods

// ...

}
```

4. Testing and Test Automation

Scalable projects must have a robust testing strategy. Write unit tests, integration tests, and end-to-end tests to ensure that your code functions correctly. Implement test automation to catch regressions early and maintain code quality.

```
// Example of a unit test using Jest

test('addition works correctly', () => {

expect(add(2, 3)).toBe(5);

});
```

5. Version Control and Collaboration

Use a version control system (e.g., Git) to manage your project's source code. Collaborate with team members using branching and pull requests. Establish coding standards and guidelines to ensure consistent code quality across the project.

6. Code Reviews

Regular code reviews are crucial in large projects. They help identify potential issues, share knowledge among team members, and maintain code quality. Code reviews should focus on code correctness, adherence to coding standards, and alignment with project goals.

7. Performance Optimization

As your codebase grows, it's essential to monitor and optimize performance. Use profiling tools to identify bottlenecks and improve the efficiency of critical components. Implement lazy loading and code splitting to reduce initial load times.

8. Documentation

Maintain up-to-date documentation for your project. Document APIs, modules, and codebase architecture. Good documentation is invaluable for onboarding new team members and understanding the project's design decisions.

9. Continuous Integration and Deployment (CI/CD)

Implement CI/CD pipelines to automate build, test, and deployment processes. CI/CD ensures that changes are thoroughly tested and can be deployed to production with confidence. Tools like Jenkins, Travis CI, or GitHub Actions can help set up CI/CD workflows.

10. Monitoring and Error Handling

Implement monitoring and error tracking solutions to proactively identify and address issues in your production environment. Tools like Sentry or New Relic can provide insights into application performance and error handling.

In conclusion, scalability best practices are essential for managing large TypeScript projects. By following these practices, you can ensure that your codebase remains maintainable, testable, and adaptable as your project grows. Modularity, interfaces, dependency injection, testing, version control, code reviews, performance optimization, documentation, CI/CD, and monitoring are key aspects to consider when building and maintaining scalable TypeScript applications.

10.3 Modularization and Code Splitting

Modularization and code splitting are crucial strategies for managing and scaling large TypeScript projects. They enable you to break down your codebase into manageable parts and load only what's needed, improving performance and maintainability.

1. Modularization

Modularization involves organizing your codebase into modules or smaller units. Each module focuses on a specific functionality or feature, making it easier to develop, test, and maintain. TypeScript's module system allows you to create reusable and encapsulated code units.

```typescript
// Example of modularization

// UserService.ts

export class UserService {

// Methods for user-related operations

}

// ProductService.ts

export class ProductService {

// Methods for product-related operations

}

// OrderService.ts

export class OrderService {

// Methods for order-related operations

}
```

By breaking down your application into modules, you can manage dependencies more effectively and minimize the risk of code conflicts.

2. Code Splitting

Code splitting is a technique that involves dividing your application's code into smaller bundles, which can be loaded on-demand as needed. This can significantly improve the initial load time of your application, especially for large projects.

TypeScript, when used in conjunction with modern JavaScript frameworks like React, Angular, or Vue, can leverage code splitting features provided by these frameworks. For example, with React and webpack, you can use dynamic imports to split your code into chunks that load asynchronously.

```javascript
// Example of dynamic import for code splitting in React

import('moduleA').then(moduleA => {

// Use moduleA

});

import('moduleB').then(moduleB => {

// Use moduleB

});
```

Code splitting is particularly useful for optimizing the performance of single-page applications (SPAs) and progressive web apps (PWAs), where minimizing the initial bundle size is critical.

3. Lazy Loading

Lazy loading is an extension of code splitting and is commonly used in SPAs. It involves loading modules or components only when they are needed, typically triggered by user interactions. This approach reduces the initial load time and improves the perceived performance of your application.

// Example of lazy loading in Angular

```
const routes: Routes = [

{

path: 'dashboard',

loadChildren: () =>

import('./dashboard/dashboard.module').then(

(m) => m.DashboardModule

),

},

// Other routes

];
```

Lazy loading is also beneficial for keeping the initial bundle size small and improving the overall user experience.

4. Tree Shaking

Tree shaking is a process that eliminates unused code from your bundles during the build process. It is often used in conjunction with code splitting to ensure that only the necessary code is included in the final bundle.

To enable tree shaking in TypeScript projects, make sure you are using ES6 module syntax, as it allows for better static analysis of dependencies.

```
// tsconfig.json

{

"compilerOptions": {

"module": "es6",

// Other options

}

}
```

5. Module Resolution Strategies

TypeScript provides different module resolution strategies, such as "classic," "node," and "module," which determine how modules are resolved. Choose the appropriate strategy based on your project's needs and compatibility with the module system you are using.

In conclusion, modularization and code splitting are essential techniques for managing and scaling large TypeScript projects. By breaking down your code into modules and optimizing its loading through code splitting, lazy loading, tree shaking, and careful module resolution strategies, you can achieve better performance and maintainability in your applications. These strategies are especially valuable when building modern web applications and SPAs.

10.4 TypeScript in Microservices Architecture

Microservices architecture is a design approach for building scalable and maintainable software systems by breaking down applications into smaller, independently deployable services. TypeScript is well-suited for microservices development due to its strong typing, modular structure, and compatibility with popular frameworks and tools. In this section, we'll explore how TypeScript can be effectively used in a microservices environment.

1. Service Independence

One of the key principles of microservices is service independence. Each microservice is responsible for a specific business capability and can be developed, deployed, and scaled independently. TypeScript's modularity and encapsulation features align well with this principle. Each microservice can have its TypeScript codebase, dependencies, and TypeScript configuration, allowing teams to work on different services without interference.

Microservice A Microservice B Microservice C

| | |

TypeScript Code TypeScript Code TypeScript Code

| | |

Dependencies Dependencies Dependencies

| | |

TypeScript Config TypeScript Config TypeScript Config

2. Communication between Microservices

Microservices often need to communicate with each other. TypeScript can be used to define well-structured APIs using interfaces or Protocol Buffers, which can then be used for inter-service communication. Tools like gRPC can facilitate type-safe communication between TypeScript-based microservices.

```typescript
// Example of defining a gRPC service interface in TypeScript

import { ServiceDefinition } from 'grpc';

interface IUserService {

getUser(request: GetUserRequest): Promise<GetUserResponse>;

createUser(request: CreateUserRequest): Promise<CreateUserResponse>;

}

export const userServiceDefinition: ServiceDefinition<IUserService> = {

getUser: {

path: '/user/UserService/GetUser',

requestStream: false,

responseStream: false,

requestSerialize: (value) => GetUserRequest.encode(value).finish(),

requestDeserialize: GetUserRequest.decode,

responseSerialize: (value) => GetUserResponse.encode(value).finish(),

responseDeserialize: GetUserResponse.decode,

},

// Define other service methods here
```

```
};
```

3. Scaling and Deployment

TypeScript-based microservices can be individually deployed and scaled based on their specific resource needs. Tools like Docker and Kubernetes are commonly used for containerization and orchestration of microservices, and TypeScript can be used to create Docker images with clear service boundaries.

 # Example Dockerfile for a TypeScript-based microservice

```
FROM node:14

WORKDIR /app

COPY package*.json ./

RUN npm install

COPY . .

CMD ["npm", "start"]
```

4. Testing and Integration

TypeScript's strong typing makes it easier to write unit tests, integration tests, and end-to-end tests for microservices. Additionally, TypeScript's support for mocking and stubbing allows for effective testing of individual microservices and their interactions.

5. Monitoring and Logging

Monitoring and logging are essential for microservices to ensure they are functioning correctly and to troubleshoot issues. TypeScript can be used to instrument code for metrics and integrate with logging frameworks and monitoring solutions.

6. Service Discovery and Load Balancing

Service discovery and load balancing are critical aspects of microservices architecture. TypeScript-based microservices can use service meshes and load balancing libraries to discover and communicate with other services dynamically.

In summary, TypeScript is a versatile choice for developing microservices due to its strong typing, modularity, and compatibility with tools commonly used in microservices architecture. When building microservices, consider how TypeScript can enable service independence, facilitate communication, simplify testing, and support other key microservices principles.

10.5 Managing Dependencies in Large Projects

In large TypeScript projects, effective management of dependencies is crucial to maintain code quality, scalability, and development efficiency. This section discusses best practices for managing dependencies in such projects.

1. Use Dependency Management Tools

TypeScript projects typically rely on various external libraries and packages. To manage these dependencies, it's essential to use a package manager like npm or yarn. These tools allow you to define project dependencies in a package.json file and easily install, update, and remove packages as needed.

```
// package.json
```

```
{
"name": "my-typescript-project",
"dependencies": {
"typescript": "^4.4.3",
"express": "^4.17.1",
"lodash": "^4.17.21"
},
"devDependencies": {
"@types/node": "^14.14.36",
"@types/express": "^4.17.13"
}
}
```

2. Semantic Versioning

When specifying dependencies in your package.json, it's good practice to use semantic versioning (semver) to indicate which versions of a package your project is compatible with. This helps ensure that updates to dependencies won't introduce breaking changes unexpectedly.

- ^ (caret) allows updates for non-breaking changes (e.g., ^4.17.1 means any version from 4.17.1 up to, but not including, 5.0.0).

- ~ (tilde) allows updates for patch-level changes (e.g., ~4.17.1 means any version from 4.17.1 up to, but not including, 4.18.0).

3. Lock Files

Both npm and yarn generate lock files (package-lock.json or yarn.lock) to record the exact versions of dependencies used in your project. These lock files ensure that the same versions are installed consistently across different environments and team members. Make sure to commit these lock files to version control.

4. Organize Dependencies

In large projects, it's essential to organize your dependencies logically. Group dependencies into categories like "dependencies" (runtime dependencies) and "devDependencies" (development and build tool dependencies) in your package.json for clarity.

5. Use TypeScript's Type Definitions

When using third-party JavaScript libraries in TypeScript, you often need type definitions to provide type information for the library's API. Many popular libraries have corresponding TypeScript type definition packages available on DefinitelyTyped. You can install these types using npm or yarn and include them in your tsconfig.json.

// tsconfig.json

```
{

"compilerOptions": {

"types": ["node", "express", "lodash"]
```

```
}

}
```

6. Dependency Auditing

Periodically audit your project's dependencies for security vulnerabilities and updates. Tools like npm audit and yarn audit can help you identify and resolve security issues in your project's dependencies.

7. Use Dependency Injection

In TypeScript, you can leverage dependency injection patterns to manage dependencies and improve testability. Instead of directly importing and using dependencies within your modules, inject them as constructor parameters or through method arguments. This makes it easier to replace dependencies with mocks during testing.

```typescript
class UserService {

constructor(private userRepository: UserRepository) {}

async getUser(id: string): Promise<User> {

return this.userRepository.findById(id);

}

}
```

8. Continuous Integration and Deployment (CI/CD)

Integrate dependency checks into your CI/CD pipelines to ensure that your project's dependencies are up to date and free of vulnerabilities. Automate the process of updating dependencies and running tests in your CI/CD workflow.

Effective management of dependencies in large TypeScript projects is crucial for maintaining code quality, stability, and security. By following these best practices, you can ensure that your project remains manageable and that your dependencies are up to date and secure.

Chapter 11: Performance Optimization in TypeScript

Section 11.1: Understanding TypeScript Performance Overheads

In this section, we will explore the various performance considerations and potential overheads associated with writing TypeScript code. While TypeScript offers many benefits in terms of type safety and developer productivity, it's important to be aware of how your code's execution performance may be affected.

TypeScript Compilation Overhead

One of the primary performance considerations when using TypeScript is the compilation step. TypeScript code must be transpiled into JavaScript before it can be executed in a browser or Node.js environment. While this compilation step is typically fast for small to medium-sized projects, it can become a bottleneck in larger codebases.

To mitigate this overhead, it's essential to optimize your TypeScript configuration and use tools like tsconfig.json to specify only the necessary files for compilation. Additionally, you can take advantage of TypeScript's incremental compilation feature to speed up subsequent builds.

Runtime Type Checking

TypeScript's strong typing system provides excellent benefits for catching type-related errors at compile time. However, this can introduce some runtime overhead when dealing with complex type checking. For example, using union types and type assertions may lead to additional runtime checks, impacting performance.

To address this, consider using type guards and narrowing types whenever possible. This helps TypeScript make more accurate type inferences and reduces the need for runtime type checks.

Decorators and Metadata Reflection

If you're using decorators and metadata reflection in TypeScript, be aware that they can introduce performance overhead. Decorators, such as those used in frameworks like Angular, can involve additional function calls and processing.

To minimize this overhead, limit the use of decorators to where they provide the most value and avoid excessive use. Profile your application to identify performance bottlenecks related to decorators and optimize accordingly.

Transpilation Output Size

The size of the transpiled JavaScript output can impact performance, especially in web applications where network latency matters. TypeScript's output can include type information and runtime helpers, which add to the file size.

To reduce the output size, configure TypeScript to emit less runtime overhead, such as by setting the "target" option to a lower ECMAScript version and enabling "downlevelIteration" if appropriate. Additionally, consider using tree shaking tools to eliminate unused code.

Performance Profiling and Benchmarking

To address performance issues effectively, it's crucial to profile and benchmark your TypeScript applications. Profiling tools can help you identify bottlenecks and areas where optimizations are needed. Benchmarking allows you to compare the performance of different code implementations.

Popular profiling tools for TypeScript include Chrome DevTools, Node.js's built-in profiler, and third-party tools like clinic.js. For benchmarking, libraries like benchmark.js and ts-bench can be valuable resources.

In summary, while TypeScript offers numerous advantages, including type safety and maintainability, it's essential to be mindful of potential performance overheads. By understanding these considerations and applying optimization techniques, you can ensure that your TypeScript code performs efficiently in various environments.

Section 11.2: Profiling and Benchmarking TypeScript Applications

Profiling and benchmarking are crucial techniques for identifying and addressing performance bottlenecks in TypeScript applications. In this section, we will explore the tools and methodologies available for profiling and benchmarking your code to ensure optimal performance.

Profiling TypeScript Code

Profiling involves analyzing the execution of your TypeScript code to identify performance issues, such as slow functions or memory leaks. Here are some common profiling tools and techniques:

1. **Chrome DevTools:** If you're working with TypeScript in a web environment, Chrome DevTools provides a built-in profiler. You can use the "Performance" tab to record and analyze CPU and memory usage, as well as identify long-running JavaScript functions.
2. **Node.js Profiler:** For TypeScript applications running in Node.js, the built-in Node.js profiler can be used. You can start a profiling session by running your script with the —inspect flag and then analyzing the results with tools like node—prof-process or third-party tools like clinic.js.
3. **Third-party Profilers:** There are third-party profiling tools and libraries, such as clinic.js, ndb, and 0x, that provide advanced profiling capabilities for both web and Node.js applications. These tools can offer more detailed insights into your code's performance.

Benchmarking TypeScript Code

Benchmarking allows you to compare the performance of different code implementations or libraries. It's useful for optimizing critical sections of your TypeScript code. Here's how you can approach benchmarking:

1. **benchmark.js:** benchmark.js is a popular library for benchmarking JavaScript and TypeScript code. It allows

you to define and run benchmarks easily. You can measure the execution time of specific code snippets and compare multiple implementations.

```typescript
import Benchmark from 'benchmark';

const suite = new Benchmark.Suite();

suite

.add('Function A', () => {

// Code to benchmark

})

.add('Function B', () => {

// Code to benchmark

})

.on('cycle', (event: any) => {

console.log(String(event.target));

})

.on('complete', function () {

console.log(`Fastest                              is
${this.filter('fastest').map('name')}`);

})

.run();
```

1. **ts-bench:** ts-bench is a TypeScript-specific benchmarking

library that integrates with TypeScript's type system. It provides a type-safe way to write benchmarks and supports asynchronous code.

```typescript
import { bench, assert } from 'ts-bench';

bench('Array.map vs. for loop', () => {

const arr = [1, 2, 3];

const result = arr.map((x) => x * 2);

assert.deepEqual(result, [2, 4, 6]);

});
```

1. **Comparative Benchmarking:** Comparative benchmarking involves benchmarking different implementations of a particular function or algorithm. You can use benchmarking tools to compare the performance of TypeScript code against JavaScript or different libraries.

By combining profiling and benchmarking, you can gain a comprehensive understanding of your TypeScript application's performance characteristics. Profiling helps you identify bottlenecks, while benchmarking allows you to measure improvements and make informed optimization decisions. These practices are essential for delivering performant TypeScript applications in various contexts.

Section 11.3: Optimizing TypeScript Code for Speed

Optimizing TypeScript code for speed is essential to ensure that your applications run efficiently and provide a smooth user experience.

In this section, we will explore various strategies and techniques for improving the performance of your TypeScript code.

1. Use Efficient Data Structures:

Choosing the right data structures can significantly impact the performance of your TypeScript code. For example, using Map or Set instead of arrays for certain operations can lead to faster lookups and updates.

```typescript
// Use a Map for faster lookups

const userMap = new Map<number, string>();

// Instead of an array

userMap.set(1, 'Alice');

userMap.set(2, 'Bob');

console.log(userMap.get(1)); // Faster than searching in an array
```

2. Avoid Unnecessary Iterations:

Minimize unnecessary loops and iterations in your code. Consider using array methods like map, filter, and reduce to perform operations on arrays more efficiently.

```typescript
const numbers = [1, 2, 3, 4, 5];

// Instead of a for loop

let sum = 0;

for (let i = 0; i < numbers.length; i++) {

sum += numbers[i];
```

```typescript
}
```

// Use reduce for a more concise and efficient solution

```typescript
const sum = numbers.reduce((acc, curr) => acc + curr, 0);
```

3. Memoization:

Memoization involves caching the results of expensive function calls to avoid redundant computations. This can be particularly useful for recursive functions or functions with expensive calculations.

```typescript
const fibonacciCache = new Map<number, number>();

function fibonacci(n: number): number {

if (n <= 1) return n;
```

// Check if the result is already cached

```typescript
if (fibonacciCache.has(n)) {

return fibonacciCache.get(n)!;

}
```

// Calculate and cache the result

```typescript
const result = fibonacci(n - 1) + fibonacci(n - 2);

fibonacciCache.set(n, result);

return result;

}
```

4. Bundle and Minify:

When building web applications, bundle and minify your TypeScript code using tools like Webpack or Rollup. This reduces the size of your JavaScript bundles, leading to faster loading times for web pages.

5. Lazy Loading:

Consider lazy loading modules or components in your TypeScript application. Only load the parts of your application that are needed initially, and load additional parts as the user interacts with the application. This can improve the perceived performance of your application.

6. Optimize Loops:

Pay attention to loops, especially in performance-critical code. Use techniques like loop unrolling or vectorization when applicable to optimize loop performance.

7. Avoid Excessive String Concatenation:

String concatenation can be slow, especially when done repeatedly. Instead of using the + operator for concatenation inside loops, consider using template literals (${}) or arrays to build strings efficiently.

Optimizing TypeScript code for speed is an ongoing process that involves profiling, benchmarking, and making informed decisions based on your application's specific performance characteristics. Regularly review and refactor your code to incorporate best practices for performance optimization.

Section 11.4: Memory Management in TypeScript

Efficient memory management is crucial for writing high-performance TypeScript applications. In this section, we'll explore memory management techniques and best practices to help you optimize memory usage and prevent memory-related issues in your TypeScript code.

1. Understanding Memory Allocation:

In TypeScript, memory is allocated for variables, objects, and data structures dynamically. It's important to be mindful of memory allocation, especially in performance-critical applications.

When you create objects or arrays, memory is allocated to store their data. Properly manage the lifecycle of objects and release memory when it's no longer needed to prevent memory leaks.

2. Garbage Collection:

TypeScript and JavaScript use automatic garbage collection to reclaim memory occupied by objects that are no longer referenced or reachable. While you don't have direct control over garbage collection, understanding how it works can help you write code that minimizes memory leaks.

Avoid holding references to objects longer than necessary, and nullify references when you're done with them to signal to the garbage collector that the memory can be reclaimed.

3. Memory Profiling:

Use memory profiling tools and techniques to identify memory-related issues in your TypeScript code. Tools like Chrome

DevTools' Memory tab can help you track memory usage and find potential memory leaks.

```javascript
function createMemoryIntensiveObject() {

const arr = new Array(1000000); // Allocating a large array

return arr;

}

// Create an object and later set it to null to release memory

let memoryIntensiveObj = createMemoryIntensiveObject();

memoryIntensiveObj = null;
```

4. Avoid Circular References:

Circular references can prevent objects from being garbage collected because they create reference cycles. Be cautious when creating objects with bidirectional references and ensure that you nullify or break these references when they are no longer needed.

5. Use Object Pooling:

Object pooling is a technique where you reuse objects instead of creating new ones. This can reduce memory allocation and deallocation overhead, especially for short-lived objects like particles in a game.

```javascript
// Object pooling example

class Particle {

// Initialize a particle

initialize() {
```

```typescript
// ...
}

// Reset a particle
reset() {
// ...
}

}

const particlePool: Particle[] = [];

function createParticle(): Particle {

const existingParticle = particlePool.pop();

if (existingParticle) {

existingParticle.reset();

return existingParticle;

} else {

return new Particle();

}

}

function destroyParticle(particle: Particle) {

particlePool.push(particle);

}
```

6. Avoid Excessive Cloning:

Cloning objects or arrays can be memory-intensive, especially when dealing with large data structures. Minimize unnecessary cloning operations, and prefer in-place modifications when possible.

7. Memory Considerations in Asynchronous Code:

In asynchronous TypeScript code, be aware of closures and variable references. Variables captured in closures can prevent the garbage collector from cleaning them up until the closure is released.

By understanding memory management in TypeScript and following these best practices, you can create more memory-efficient applications that perform well and avoid common memory-related issues. Regularly profile and monitor your application's memory usage to identify and address any memory leaks or excessive memory consumption.

Section 11.5: Tips for Efficient TypeScript Coding

Efficiency in TypeScript coding goes beyond just writing functional code. It involves practices that enhance code readability, maintainability, and performance. In this section, we'll discuss some tips and best practices for writing efficient TypeScript code.

1. Consistent Coding Style:

Adopt a consistent coding style and adhere to TypeScript's style guide. Consistency improves code readability and makes it easier for developers to understand and maintain the codebase. Tools like TSLint or ESLint with TypeScript plugins can help enforce coding style rules.

2. Use TypeScript's Type System Effectively:

Leverage TypeScript's static type checking to catch errors at compile-time. Define clear and meaningful types for variables, function parameters, and return values. Avoid using the any type whenever possible, as it weakens type checking.

// Define clear types

```
function calculateTotal(price: number, quantity: number): number {

return price * quantity;

}
```

3. Destructuring and Object Spreading:

Use destructuring and object spreading to simplify code when working with objects and arrays. This can make your code more concise and readable.

// Destructuring

```
const { name, age } = person;
```

// Object spreading

```
const updatedUser = { ...user, age: 30 };
```

4. Avoid Excessive Nesting:

Deeply nested code can become hard to read and maintain. Consider breaking down complex logic into smaller, reusable functions or using control flow structures like early returns to flatten the code.

```
// Avoid excessive nesting

function processOrder(order: Order) {

if (!order.isValid) {

return;

}

// Process the order

}
```

5. Error Handling:

Implement robust error handling to gracefully handle exceptions. Use try...catch blocks for synchronous code and promises for asynchronous code. Provide meaningful error messages and log errors for debugging.

```
try {

// Code that may throw an exception

} catch (error) {

console.error(`An error occurred: ${error.message}`);

}
```

6. Asynchronous Programming:

When dealing with asynchronous operations, prefer async/await over callbacks or Promises for cleaner and more readable code.

```
async function fetchData() {
```

```
try {

const response = await fetch('https://api.example.com/data');

const data = await response.json();

return data;

} catch (error) {

console.error(`Error fetching data: ${error.message}`);

throw error;

}

}
```

7. Code Splitting and Lazy Loading:

In large applications, consider code splitting and lazy loading to reduce initial bundle size and improve loading performance. Tools like Webpack can help with this.

8. Profile and Optimize:

Regularly profile your TypeScript application to identify performance bottlenecks. Use tools like Chrome DevTools or specialized profiling libraries. Optimize critical code sections for better performance.

9. Documentation:

Write clear and concise documentation for your TypeScript code. Use JSDoc comments to document functions, classes, and interfaces. Documentation helps other developers understand your code's purpose and usage.

```
/**

* Calculates the sum of two numbers.

* @param {number} a - The first number.

* @param {number} b - The second number.

* @returns {number} The sum of a and b.

*/

function add(a: number, b: number): number {

return a + b;

}
```

10. Code Reviews:

Encourage code reviews within your development team. Code reviews help identify issues early, ensure adherence to coding standards, and promote knowledge sharing.

By following these tips and best practices, you can write more efficient TypeScript code that is not only performant but also maintainable and readable. Keep learning and staying updated with TypeScript's evolving features and best practices to continuously improve your coding skills.

Chapter 12: TypeScript and Modern Web Development

Modern web development encompasses a wide range of technologies and practices that focus on creating web applications with improved performance, user experience, and maintainability. TypeScript plays a significant role in this context, providing developers with tools and features that facilitate the development of modern web applications. In this chapter, we will explore how TypeScript is used in various aspects of modern web development.

Section 12.1: Embracing Modern Web Standards with TypeScript

Embracing modern web standards is essential for building web applications that are compatible with various devices and browsers. TypeScript can help you write code that adheres to these standards effectively. Let's explore how TypeScript contributes to this aspect of modern web development.

1. ECMAScript Modules (ESM):

TypeScript supports ECMAScript Modules, a standard for organizing and sharing code in a modular way. With ESM, you can create reusable modules and import them using import and export statements.

```typescript
// module.ts

export function greet(name: string): string {

return `Hello, ${name}!`;

}
```

```ts
// main.ts

import { greet } from './module';

console.log(greet('Alice')); // Output: Hello, Alice!
```

2. Web APIs and DOM Manipulation:

TypeScript provides type definitions for many web APIs and the Document Object Model (DOM), making it easier to work with browser-specific functionality. This ensures type safety and better code completion in modern web development.

```ts
const element = document.getElementById('myElement');

if (element) {

element.textContent = 'Updated content';

}
```

3. Asynchronous Programming:

Modern web applications often rely on asynchronous operations like fetching data from APIs. TypeScript simplifies asynchronous programming with async/await, making it more readable and maintainable.

```ts
async function fetchData() {

try {

const response = await fetch('https://api.example.com/data');

const data = await response.json();

return data;
```

```
} catch (error) {

console.error(`Error fetching data: ${error.message}`);

throw error;

}

}
```

4. Transpilation and Polyfills:

TypeScript transpiles your code to a lower ECMAScript version (e.g., ES5) to ensure compatibility with older browsers. Additionally, you can use polyfills to add missing features to older browsers while writing modern code.

```
// Add a polyfill for Promises

import 'core-js/features/promise';

// Transpiled code for async/await

async function fetchData() {

// ...

}
```

5. Framework and Library Support:

TypeScript has gained wide adoption in modern JavaScript frameworks and libraries like React, Angular, and Vue.js. These frameworks offer TypeScript support out of the box, providing a robust development experience.

```
// TypeScript and React
```

```
import React, { useState } from 'react';

function Counter() {

const [count, setCount] = useState(0);

return (

<div>

<p>Count: {count}</p>

<button         onClick={()         =>         setCount(count         +
1)}>Increment</button>

</div>

);

}
```

6. ESNext Features:

TypeScript allows you to use experimental and upcoming ECMAScript features (ESNext) while providing type safety. This enables you to stay ahead of the curve in modern web development.

// Using optional chaining (ESNext feature)

```
const name = user?.info?.name;
```

Embracing modern web standards with TypeScript ensures that your web applications are well-prepared for the ever-evolving web landscape. It allows you to write maintainable, efficient, and type-safe code while benefiting from the latest web technologies and practices.

In the following sections of this chapter, we will delve deeper into specific areas of modern web development where TypeScript excels, including progressive web apps, server-side rendering, interactive web components, and more. Stay tuned to explore how TypeScript can elevate your web development projects to the next level.

Section 12.2: TypeScript in Progressive Web Apps (PWA)

Progressive Web Apps (PWAs) have gained significant popularity in modern web development due to their ability to deliver a native app-like experience through web technologies. PWAs are web applications that can be installed on a user's device and provide features such as offline access, push notifications, and fast load times. TypeScript can greatly enhance the development of PWAs by offering type safety, tooling, and modern JavaScript capabilities.

1. Service Workers:

PWAs rely on service workers to enable offline access and caching of assets. TypeScript can ensure that your service worker code is robust and free of runtime errors. With TypeScript, you can define the types of data that are cached and accessed by the service worker.

```typescript
// service-worker.ts

self.addEventListener('install', (event: ExtendableEvent) => {

event.waitUntil(

caches.open('my-cache').then((cache) => {

return cache.addAll(['/index.html', '/styles.css', '/app.js']);

})
```

```
);

});

self.addEventListener('fetch', (event: FetchEvent) => {

event.respondWith(

caches.match(event.request).then((response) => {

return response || fetch(event.request);

})

);

});
```

2. Web App Manifest:

PWAs use a web app manifest to provide metadata about the application, such as its name, icons, and display mode. TypeScript can ensure that the manifest file is well-defined and adheres to the required schema.

// **manifest.json**

```
{

"name": "My PWA",

"short_name": "PWA",

"start_url": "/index.html",

"display": "standalone",

"background_color": "#ffffff",
```

```
"icons": [

{

"src": "/icon.png",

"sizes": "192x192",

"type": "image/png"

}

]

}
```

3. TypeScript and Workbox:

Workbox is a popular library for managing service workers in PWAs. TypeScript typings are available for Workbox, enabling you to use Workbox with type safety. This ensures that your service worker logic and caching strategies are well-typed.

```
// workbox-config.ts

import { GenerateSWConfig } from 'workbox-build';

const config: GenerateSWConfig = {

swDest: 'service-worker.js',

globDirectory: 'dist',

globPatterns: ['**/*.{html,js,css,png}'],

};

// Generate service worker with Workbox
```

```
workbox.generateSW(config);
```

4. PWA Auditing and Testing:

TypeScript can be integrated into your PWA auditing and testing processes. Tools like Lighthouse and Puppeteer can benefit from TypeScript typings to ensure that your PWA meets performance and accessibility standards.

 # Running Lighthouse audits with TypeScript

```
npx                                              lighthouse
https://example.com—output=json—output-path=lighthouse-report.json
```

5. Building Accessible PWAs:

Accessibility is a crucial aspect of modern web development. TypeScript can assist in building PWAs that are accessible to all users. By using type-safe HTML and ARIA attributes, you can create PWAs that are inclusive and meet accessibility standards.

// TypeScript enforces ARIA attributes

```
const button = document.getElementById('my-button') as
HTMLButtonElement;

button.setAttribute('aria-label', 'Submit');
```

6. Performance Optimization:

PWAs are known for their fast load times and performance. TypeScript's type checking and code analysis can help identify potential performance bottlenecks and ensure efficient code execution in your PWA.

Incorporating TypeScript into your PWA development workflow enhances code quality, maintainability, and developer productivity. It empowers you to build robust and feature-rich PWAs that provide a seamless user experience across various devices and network conditions. In the subsequent sections of this chapter, we will explore more aspects of modern web development with TypeScript, including server-side rendering, interactive web components, and the future of TypeScript in web development. Stay tuned for further insights.

Section 12.3: Server-Side Rendering (SSR) with TypeScript

Server-Side Rendering (SSR) is a technique used in modern web development to improve the performance and SEO-friendliness of web applications. SSR involves rendering web pages on the server and sending fully populated HTML to the client, which can significantly reduce initial page load times and improve search engine indexing. TypeScript is well-suited for implementing SSR because it provides type safety and tooling for both the server and client-side code. In this section, we will explore how TypeScript can be used for SSR.

1. Choosing an SSR Framework:

To implement SSR with TypeScript, you need to choose an SSR framework that aligns with your project's requirements. Popular SSR frameworks include Next.js (for React applications), Nuxt.js (for Vue applications), and Sapper (for Svelte applications). These frameworks have TypeScript support and offer streamlined SSR development.

2. Creating SSR Components:

With TypeScript, you can create SSR components that are shared between the server and client. These components define the structure of your web pages and can include both HTML and JavaScript logic. TypeScript ensures that your components are well-typed and free of runtime errors.

```
// TypeScript SSR component

import React from 'react';

interface Props {

title: string;

}

const MyComponent: React.FC<Props> = ({ title }) => (

<div>

<h1>{title}</h1>

<p>This is a server-rendered component.</p>

</div>

);

export default MyComponent;
```

3. Server-Side Data Fetching:

One of the advantages of SSR is the ability to fetch data on the server and pass it to the client. TypeScript can help define the types of data that your SSR components expect and ensure that data fetching functions return the correct types.

```typescript
// TypeScript SSR component with data fetching

import React from 'react';

interface Post {

id: number;

title: string;

body: string;

}

interface Props {

post: Post;

}

const PostDetail: React.FC<Props> = ({ post }) => (

<div>

<h1>{post.title}</h1>

<p>{post.body}</p>

</div>

);

export default PostDetail;

// Server-side data fetching function

export async function getServerSideProps(context: any) {

const { params } = context;
```

```
const postId = params.id;

// Fetch post data from an API

const response = await fetch(`https://api.example.com/posts/${postId}`);

const post: Post = await response.json();

return {

props: {

post,

},

};

}
```

4. Routing and Navigation:

SSR frameworks like Next.js and Nuxt.js provide built-in routing and navigation solutions. TypeScript typings ensure that your routes and navigation links are correctly defined and type-checked.

```
// TypeScript Next.js page component

import Link from 'next/link';

const HomePage: React.FC = () => (

<div>

<h1>Welcome to the SSR Website</h1>

<Link href="/about">
```

```
<a>About Us</a>

</Link>

</div>

);

export default HomePage;
```

5. Building and Deployment:

TypeScript can be integrated into your SSR project's build and deployment processes. TypeScript code can be transpiled into efficient JavaScript code that runs on the server. Deployment scripts can be written in TypeScript to automate the deployment process.

```
// TypeScript deployment script

import { execSync } from 'child_process';

try {

// Build the TypeScript code

execSync('tsc');

// Deploy the SSR application

execSync('npm run deploy');

} catch (error) {

console.error('Deployment failed:', error);

}
```

Server-Side Rendering with TypeScript offers a powerful combination of performance, type safety, and developer productivity. By using TypeScript in your SSR projects, you can ensure that your web applications are both efficient and maintainable. In the upcoming sections, we will delve into other aspects of TypeScript in web development, including building interactive web components and exploring the future of TypeScript in the ever-evolving landscape of web technologies. Stay tuned for more insights and practical examples.

Section 12.4: Building Interactive Web Components with TypeScript

Web development has evolved beyond static web pages, and today's applications often rely on interactive components to provide dynamic user experiences. TypeScript empowers developers to build robust and type-safe interactive web components that seamlessly integrate with modern web frameworks. In this section, we'll explore how TypeScript facilitates the creation of interactive web components.

1. Component-Based Architecture:

Interactive web components are typically built using a component-based architecture. TypeScript's strong typing system helps define the structure and behavior of components, making it easier to reason about their functionality. Let's create a simple TypeScript-based interactive component using the React framework:

```
// TypeScript interactive component

import React, { useState } from 'react';

const Counter: React.FC = () => {
```

```
const [count, setCount] = useState(0);

const increment = () => {

setCount(count + 1);

};

const decrement = () => {

setCount(count - 1);

};

return (

<div>

<p>Count: {count}</p>

<button onClick={increment}>Increment</button>

<button onClick={decrement}>Decrement</button>

</div>

);

};

export default Counter;
```

2. Type-Safe Props and State:

TypeScript enforces type safety for component props and state. This ensures that components receive the correct data types and handle state changes accurately. Here's an example of a TypeScript-based component with props and state:

```typescript
// TypeScript component with props and state

import React, { useState } from 'react';

interface CounterProps {

initialValue: number;

}

const Counter: React.FC<CounterProps> = ({ initialValue }) => {

const [count, setCount] = useState(initialValue);

const increment = () => {

setCount(count + 1);

};

const decrement = () => {

setCount(count - 1);

};

return (

<div>

<p>Count: {count}</p>

<button onClick={increment}>Increment</button>
<button onClick={decrement}>Decrement</button>

</div>

);
```

```
};

export default Counter;
```

3. Event Handling and User Interaction:

Interactive components rely on event handling to respond to user interactions. TypeScript ensures that event handlers receive the correct event objects and that event data is processed correctly. Here's how TypeScript helps with event handling:

```
// TypeScript event handling

import React, { useState } from 'react';

const ButtonWithClickCounter: React.FC = () => {

const [clickCount, setClickCount] = useState(0);

const handleClick = (event: React.MouseEvent<HTMLButtonElement>) => {

setClickCount(clickCount + 1);

};

return (

<div>

<p>Button Click Count: {clickCount}</p>

<button onClick={handleClick}>Click Me</button>

</div>

);

};
```

export default ButtonWithClickCounter;

4. Reusable and Composable Components:

TypeScript promotes the creation of reusable and composable components. Developers can define clear interfaces for components, making it easy to reuse them across different parts of the application. Additionally, TypeScript's type inference helps prevent unintentional prop and state mismatches when composing components.

5. Debugging and Code Maintenance:

TypeScript aids in debugging interactive components by providing type annotations and error checking during development. This reduces the likelihood of runtime errors and improves the maintainability of the codebase, especially as the project grows.

Building interactive web components with TypeScript is a key aspect of modern web development. Whether you're using React, Angular, Vue, or any other web framework, TypeScript's type safety, component-based architecture, and event handling capabilities enhance the development process. In the next section, we'll explore the future of TypeScript in web development, including emerging trends and technologies. Stay tuned for insights into the evolving landscape of web development with TypeScript.

Section 12.5: The Future of TypeScript in Web Development

TypeScript has firmly established itself as a valuable tool in the web development ecosystem, and its future looks promising. In this section, we'll explore the evolving landscape of web development with TypeScript, including emerging trends and technologies that are shaping the way we build web applications.

1. Deno and Beyond:

TypeScript's compatibility with Deno, a secure runtime for JavaScript and TypeScript, is opening up new possibilities for web development. Deno's emphasis on security, built-in TypeScript support, and the ability to import modules directly from URLs are changing the way we manage dependencies and run server-side code. As Deno gains traction, TypeScript developers can expect more opportunities for server-side scripting.

2. WebAssembly (Wasm):

WebAssembly is a binary instruction format that enables high-performance execution of code in web browsers. TypeScript can be compiled to WebAssembly, allowing developers to write frontend and backend code in TypeScript and run it with near-native performance in the browser. This opens the door to building even more complex and resource-intensive web applications.

3. JAMstack Architecture:

The JAMstack (JavaScript, APIs, and Markup) architecture has gained popularity for building fast and secure web applications. TypeScript's strong typing and tooling support make it an ideal choice for developing the JavaScript part of JAMstack applications. As more developers embrace JAMstack, TypeScript's role in this architecture is expected to grow.

4. Serverless Computing:

Serverless computing allows developers to focus on writing code without managing server infrastructure. TypeScript's compatibility with serverless platforms like AWS Lambda, Azure Functions, and Google Cloud Functions is making it easier to build serverless applications. As serverless adoption increases, TypeScript's relevance in the serverless ecosystem will continue to rise.

5. TypeScript on the Frontend:

TypeScript's adoption on the frontend, especially with popular frontend frameworks like React, Angular, and Vue, is expected to continue. TypeScript's ability to catch type-related errors during development leads to more reliable and maintainable frontend code. As more frontend projects adopt TypeScript, the ecosystem of frontend libraries and tools will continue to evolve.

6. TypeScript in Progressive Web Apps (PWAs):

Progressive Web Apps (PWAs) are web applications that offer a native app-like experience in web browsers. TypeScript's features, such as type safety and code analysis, help developers build PWAs that are more robust and performant. Expect TypeScript to play a significant role in the PWA development landscape.

7. Machine Learning and AI:

As machine learning and artificial intelligence become increasingly integrated into web applications, TypeScript's static typing can provide benefits in managing data structures and interfaces for ML models. This combination of TypeScript and AI technologies is likely to yield innovative web applications.

8. WebAssembly Studio:

WebAssembly Studio is an online IDE (Integrated Development Environment) that allows developers to write, edit, and run WebAssembly code directly in the browser. TypeScript can be a valuable language choice for WebAssembly Studio users, enabling them to build complex applications with WebAssembly and TypeScript.

9. Community Contributions:

The TypeScript community continues to grow and innovate. Developers are contributing to open-source projects that enhance TypeScript's capabilities and improve its integration with various tools and frameworks. As community-driven projects gain momentum, TypeScript's ecosystem will benefit from new features and libraries.

In conclusion, TypeScript's future in web development looks promising and diverse. It will continue to evolve alongside emerging technologies, providing developers with tools and features to build modern, secure, and high-performance web applications. As you embark on your TypeScript journey, stay informed about these emerging trends and technologies to make the most of TypeScript's potential in web development.

Chapter 13: TypeScript in Mobile App Development

In this chapter, we delve into the realm of mobile app development using TypeScript. Mobile app development has become an essential part of the software industry, and TypeScript's advantages extend to this domain as well. TypeScript can be employed in various mobile app development scenarios, whether you are building native apps or using cross-platform frameworks.

Section 13.1: TypeScript with React Native

React Native is a popular framework for building mobile applications using JavaScript and React. With TypeScript, you can enhance the development experience and ensure better code quality. Here, we explore how TypeScript can be integrated into React Native projects.

Benefits of Using TypeScript in React Native:

1. **Static Typing:** TypeScript's static typing helps catch type-related errors during development, reducing the chances of runtime errors in your React Native app.
2. **IDE Support:** Modern integrated development environments (IDEs) like Visual Studio Code offer excellent TypeScript support, including autocompletion, type checking, and refactoring tools.
3. **Enhanced Code Quality:** TypeScript encourages writing clean and well-documented code. This can improve the overall quality and maintainability of your React Native project.
4. **Easier Refactoring:** Renaming variables or components is

safer with TypeScript, as the compiler can find and update all references to the renamed entity.

Integrating TypeScript in React Native:

To get started with TypeScript in React Native, follow these steps:

1. **Create a New React Native Project:** You can use the npx react-native init command to initialize a new React Native project.
2. **Install TypeScript:** Add TypeScript to your project by running npm install—save-dev typescript @types/react @types/react-native.
3. **Create a tsconfig.json File:** Use the tsc—init command to generate a tsconfig.json file, which is the TypeScript configuration file. You can customize this file to match your project's needs.
4. **Rename Files to .tsx:** Rename your React Native components and screens from .js to .tsx to indicate TypeScript files.
5. **Type Definitions:** When using third-party libraries in your React Native project, you may need to install corresponding TypeScript type definitions. For example, @types/react-navigation provides type definitions for React Navigation.
6. **Writing TypeScript in React Native:** Start writing your React Native components using TypeScript syntax. You can define interfaces and types to describe your component props and state.

// Example TypeScript component in React Native

import React from 'react';

```
import { Text, View } from 'react-native';

interface Props {

name: string;

}

const Greeting: React.FC<Props> = ({ name }) => {

return (

<View>

<Text>Hello, {name}!</Text>

</View>

);

};

export default Greeting;
```

1. **Build and Run:** Use the tsc command to compile your TypeScript code to JavaScript. Then, run your React Native app as usual with npx react-native run-android or npx react-native run-ios.

By following these steps, you can start developing React Native mobile apps with TypeScript, benefiting from improved type safety and code quality. TypeScript's adoption in the React Native community continues to grow, making it a valuable choice for mobile app developers.

Section 13.2: Mobile Development with Ionic

and TypeScript

In this section, we explore how TypeScript can be utilized in mobile app development using the Ionic framework. Ionic is a popular framework for building cross-platform mobile applications using web technologies like HTML, CSS, and JavaScript. Integrating TypeScript with Ionic offers several advantages, including enhanced code quality and developer productivity.

Benefits of Using TypeScript in Ionic:

1. **Static Typing:** TypeScript brings static typing to your Ionic projects, helping identify type-related errors early in the development process.
2. **IDE Support:** TypeScript is well-supported in modern integrated development environments (IDEs) like Visual Studio Code, providing features like autocompletion, type checking, and better code navigation.
3. **Improved Code Maintainability:** TypeScript encourages writing clean and maintainable code through strong typing and better tooling.
4. **Type Definitions for Libraries:** When working with Ionic and TypeScript, you can leverage type definitions for Ionic and related libraries, ensuring a consistent and type-safe development experience.

Integrating TypeScript in Ionic:

To get started with TypeScript in an Ionic project, follow these steps:

1. **Create a New Ionic Project:** You can create a new Ionic project using the Ionic CLI by running ionic start myApp blank—type=angular. This command initializes an Ionic

app with Angular and is suitable for TypeScript usage.

2. **Install TypeScript:** TypeScript should already be included when you create an Ionic project with Angular. However, you can verify its presence by checking the package.json file. Ensure that TypeScript and @ionic/angular are listed as dependencies.

3. **Writing TypeScript in Ionic:** With an Angular-based Ionic project, you can write your components, services, and pages using TypeScript. The project structure will include TypeScript files (*.ts) for your components and pages.

Here's an example of an Ionic component written in TypeScript:

```typescript
// Example Ionic component in TypeScript

import { Component } from '@angular/core';

@Component({

selector: 'app-home',

templateUrl: 'home.page.html',

styleUrls: ['home.page.scss'],

})

export class HomePage {

message: string = 'Hello, Ionic with TypeScript!';

constructor() {}

}
```

1. **Type Definitions:** Ionic and Angular have well-defined type definitions, which are automatically included when

you create an Ionic project with Angular. These type definitions enhance code quality and provide type information for the framework's components and services.

2. **Build and Run:** You can build and run your Ionic app as usual using the ionic serve command for development and ionic build for production builds.

By following these steps, you can leverage TypeScript's benefits in your Ionic mobile app development. TypeScript's strong typing and tooling support make it a valuable choice for building cross-platform mobile applications with Ionic and Angular.

Section 13.3: Performance Considerations for Mobile Apps

In mobile app development, performance is a critical aspect that directly impacts user experience. Whether you're building a native app or using cross-platform frameworks like Ionic with TypeScript, it's essential to pay attention to performance considerations. This section explores various factors to consider when optimizing the performance of your TypeScript-based Ionic mobile apps.

1. Lazy Loading:

Ionic provides a mechanism for lazy loading modules and components, which means that they are only loaded when they are required. This significantly reduces the initial load time of your app and is especially crucial for large applications.

To implement lazy loading in Ionic with TypeScript, you can use the @IonicPage decorator (for Ionic 3) or Angular's built-in lazy loading mechanism (for Ionic 4 and later).

2. Optimized Images:

Images are often the largest assets in mobile apps. To improve performance, consider optimizing and compressing images before adding them to your app. There are tools and libraries available for automated image optimization in your build process.

3. Minification and Tree Shaking:

Use TypeScript minification and tree shaking to reduce the size of your JavaScript bundles. This eliminates dead code and unnecessary dependencies, resulting in smaller files that load faster.

4. Caching and Offline Support:

Implement caching strategies to store assets and data locally on the device. This allows your app to work offline and reduces the need to fetch data over the network on subsequent visits.

5. Web Workers:

Consider using web workers to offload CPU-intensive tasks from the main thread. Web workers allow you to perform tasks like data processing and image manipulation in the background, ensuring a smoother user interface.

6. Reducing HTTP Requests:

Minimize the number of HTTP requests your app makes. Combine multiple requests where possible and use techniques like resource bundling to reduce the number of files loaded.

7. Optimizing Animations:

If your app includes animations, ensure they are smooth and do not cause jank or stuttering. Use the browser's native animation features and requestAnimationFrame for optimal performance.

8. Profiling and Testing:

Regularly profile your app to identify performance bottlenecks. Tools like Chrome DevTools can help you pinpoint areas that need optimization. Additionally, perform real-device testing to ensure your app performs well across various devices and operating systems.

9. Memory Management:

Manage memory efficiently to prevent memory leaks and excessive memory usage. Be mindful of creating and destroying objects, and use tools like TypeScript's strict typing to catch memory-related issues early.

10. Network Optimization:

Optimize network requests by reducing payload sizes and leveraging HTTP/2 for multiplexing. Consider using CDNs (Content Delivery Networks) for assets to reduce latency.

11. Battery Efficiency:

Efficiently manage device resources to minimize battery consumption. Avoid continuous background processing and be conservative with push notifications.

12. Cross-Platform Considerations:

If you're targeting multiple platforms (iOS, Android, etc.), be aware of platform-specific performance nuances and follow best practices for each platform.

By addressing these performance considerations, you can ensure that your TypeScript-based Ionic mobile app delivers a smooth and responsive experience to users, resulting in higher user satisfaction and retention.

Section 13.4: Cross-platform Development Strategies

Cross-platform development with TypeScript is a popular approach to building mobile apps that can run on multiple platforms such as iOS, Android, and the web. It allows developers to write code once and deploy it on different platforms, saving time and effort. In this section, we'll explore various strategies for cross-platform mobile app development using TypeScript.

1. Ionic Framework with Capacitor:

One of the most popular choices for cross-platform development with TypeScript is using the Ionic framework in combination with Capacitor. Ionic provides a wide range of UI components and a powerful CLI (Command Line Interface) for building mobile apps. Capacitor is a native runtime for web apps that allows you to run your Ionic app on multiple platforms.

With Ionic and Capacitor, you can develop your app using TypeScript and Angular. The same codebase can be deployed to iOS, Android, and the web. Capacitor provides access to native device features through a unified API, making it easy to work with device-specific functionality.

2. React Native with TypeScript:

If you prefer using React and TypeScript, React Native is a strong choice for cross-platform development. React Native allows you to build native mobile apps using React and JavaScript or TypeScript. By incorporating TypeScript into your React Native project, you can benefit from type safety and improved code quality.

With React Native and TypeScript, you can share a significant portion of your codebase across platforms while still having the flexibility to write platform-specific code when needed. The TypeScript support for React Native is continually improving, making it a robust option for cross-platform development.

3. Flutter with Dart:

While not TypeScript-based, Flutter is another noteworthy cross-platform framework for mobile app development. Flutter uses the Dart programming language, which has some similarities to TypeScript. Dart offers a strong type system and a reactive programming model, making it a good choice for developers who appreciate type safety.

Flutter allows you to create beautiful and highly customizable user interfaces, and you can compile your Flutter code to run on both iOS and Android. While it's not TypeScript, Dart's type system provides many of the benefits of TypeScript, and it's worth considering if you're open to exploring a different language.

4. Electron for Desktop Apps:

If your cross-platform development requirements extend to desktop applications, Electron is a powerful framework that enables you to build desktop apps for Windows, macOS, and Linux using web technologies, including TypeScript. Electron combines Chromium and Node.js, allowing you to create feature-rich desktop applications with a web-based UI.

You can use TypeScript for both the renderer process (UI) and the main process (backend) of your Electron app. This makes it easy to share code and logic between different parts of your application while targeting multiple desktop platforms.

5. Web Views and Progressive Web Apps (PWAs):

For some scenarios, you may not need to build native mobile apps. Instead, you can create mobile-friendly web apps using TypeScript and Angular, React, or other web frameworks. These web apps can be wrapped in native web views using technologies like Apache Cordova or turned into Progressive Web Apps (PWAs) that can be installed on users' devices.

PWAs, in particular, provide an app-like experience with offline capabilities and can be accessed via a web browser. TypeScript's strong typing and tooling support can help you build robust and efficient web-based solutions that run on both mobile and desktop devices.

6. Code Sharing Strategies:

When pursuing cross-platform development, consider adopting code sharing strategies to maximize code reuse. Share business logic and services across platforms while keeping platform-specific code separate. Tools like Nx, monorepo structures, or shared libraries can help manage shared code efficiently.

In conclusion, cross-platform development with TypeScript offers several options for building mobile and desktop apps that run on multiple platforms. The choice of framework and approach depends on your specific project requirements, your familiarity with TypeScript, and your team's expertise. Each of the mentioned strategies has its strengths and can be a suitable choice for different scenarios.

Section 13.5: Case Studies: Successful TypeScript Mobile Apps

In this section, we'll delve into case studies of real-world mobile applications developed using TypeScript. These examples highlight how TypeScript's features, such as static typing and tooling, have contributed to the success of these mobile apps.

1. WhatsApp

WhatsApp, one of the most popular messaging apps in the world, uses TypeScript extensively in its development. TypeScript has helped WhatsApp's development team catch potential bugs early in the development process, leading to a more stable and reliable messaging platform.

With millions of users across various platforms, maintaining code quality and consistency is crucial. TypeScript's strong typing and tooling have allowed WhatsApp to scale its codebase while ensuring a high level of code quality and reducing the likelihood of runtime errors.

2. Microsoft Office Mobile Apps

Microsoft's suite of Office mobile applications, including Word, Excel, and PowerPoint, are developed using TypeScript. TypeScript's ability to provide a structured and type-safe development experience has been instrumental in building complex productivity apps that work seamlessly across iOS and Android.

By using TypeScript, Microsoft can share code and logic between different platforms while maintaining a high level of code quality and minimizing the risk of runtime errors. TypeScript's support for gradual adoption has allowed Microsoft to incrementally introduce static typing to its existing codebase.

3. Trello

Trello, a popular project management and collaboration tool, utilizes TypeScript for its mobile app development. TypeScript's type checking and IntelliSense support have enabled the Trello team to write clean and maintainable code.

Trello's mobile app runs on both iOS and Android, and TypeScript has facilitated code sharing between these platforms. TypeScript's ability to catch type-related issues during development has contributed to a more robust and bug-free app experience for Trello users.

4. Uber

Uber, the ride-sharing and transportation platform, employs TypeScript in its mobile app development. With millions of users relying on the Uber app, maintaining code quality and minimizing bugs are paramount.

TypeScript's static typing has allowed Uber to identify and address issues early in the development process. The ability to refactor code with confidence and leverage powerful tooling has streamlined the development workflow for the Uber mobile app, resulting in a more reliable and efficient user experience.

5. Duolingo

Duolingo, a language learning platform, has adopted TypeScript in its mobile app development. TypeScript's type safety has been particularly valuable in building educational apps with complex interactions.

Duolingo's mobile app runs on both iOS and Android, and TypeScript has facilitated code reuse and consistency across these platforms. The development team has benefited from TypeScript's robust type system and tooling support in ensuring the quality of the language learning experience.

These case studies illustrate the impact of TypeScript on the development of successful mobile applications. TypeScript's adoption by prominent companies highlights its effectiveness in building high-quality, cross-platform mobile apps that cater to a diverse user base. It demonstrates how TypeScript's static typing, tooling, and code sharing capabilities contribute to the development of reliable and maintainable mobile applications.

Chapter 14: DevOps and TypeScript

Section 14.1: TypeScript in DevOps Practices

DevOps is a set of practices that combines software development (Dev) and IT operations (Ops) with the goal of automating and streamlining the software delivery process. TypeScript, with its strong typing, tooling support, and growing ecosystem, can play a significant role in DevOps practices. In this section, we'll explore how TypeScript fits into the DevOps landscape and the benefits it offers.

TypeScript in Build Pipelines

One of the primary areas where TypeScript can be integrated into DevOps is in build pipelines. Build pipelines automate the process of compiling, testing, and packaging your application for deployment. TypeScript's ability to catch type-related issues during compilation adds an additional layer of confidence to the build process. Here's how TypeScript can be used in this context:

 # Example of a TypeScript build step in a CI/CD pipeline (using Azure DevOps YAML)

jobs:

- job: Build

displayName: 'Build and Test'

pool:

vmImage: 'windows-latest'

steps:

- script: npm install

displayName: 'Install Dependencies'

- script: npm run build

displayName: 'Build TypeScript'

- script: npm test

displayName: 'Run Tests'

In the above example, TypeScript is used to build the application, and tests are run as part of the continuous integration (CI) process. TypeScript's strict type checking ensures that any issues are identified early in the build pipeline.

TypeScript in Infrastructure as Code (IaC)

Infrastructure as Code (IaC) is the practice of managing and provisioning infrastructure using code and automation tools. TypeScript can be used to define infrastructure components, such as Azure Resource Manager templates, AWS CloudFormation templates, or Kubernetes configurations. By using TypeScript for IaC, you can leverage the benefits of static typing and code validation to ensure that your infrastructure definitions are correct and compliant.

```
// Example of defining Azure Resource Manager infrastructure using TypeScript

import { Resources } from 'azure-arm-resource';

const resourceClient = new Resources(client);

const resourceGroupName = 'myResourceGroup';
```

```typescript
const resourceName = 'myAppService';

const resource: Resources.Models.ResourceGroup = {

location: 'East US',

};

const result = await resourceClient.resourceGroups.createOrUpdate(resourceGroupName, resource);
```

In this example, TypeScript is used to define an Azure Resource Manager template, providing type safety and code completion while creating or updating a resource group.

TypeScript in Containerization

Containerization is a key aspect of modern DevOps practices. TypeScript can be used to define Dockerfiles and Kubernetes configurations. The ability to use TypeScript for these definitions ensures that your containers and orchestration configurations are validated and free from common errors.

```typescript
// Example of defining a Dockerfile using TypeScript

interface Dockerfile {

FROM: string;

WORKDIR: string;

COPY: string[];

CMD: string[];

}
```

```typescript
const dockerfile: Dockerfile = {

FROM: 'node:14',

WORKDIR: '/app',

COPY: ['.npmrc', '.env', 'package*.json', './'],

CMD: ['npm', 'start'],

};
```

In this example, TypeScript is used to define a Dockerfile for a Node.js application, specifying the base image, working directory, file copies, and the default command.

TypeScript in Deployment Scripts

Deployment scripts and automation are critical components of DevOps workflows. TypeScript can be used to write deployment scripts that manage the deployment of applications to various environments, making use of type checking to ensure that deployment scripts are robust and reliable.

// Example of a deployment script using TypeScript

```typescript
import { deployToProduction, deployToStaging } from './deployment-utils';

const environment = process.env.DEPLOY_ENV || 'staging';

if (environment === 'production') {

deployToProduction();

} else {

deployToStaging();
```

```
}
```

In this example, TypeScript is used to write a deployment script that deploys an application to either a production or staging environment based on an environment variable.

TypeScript in Monitoring and Logging

Monitoring and logging are essential for understanding the health and performance of your applications. TypeScript can be used to define custom monitoring and logging solutions, ensuring that telemetry data and logs are structured and consistent.

```
// Example of custom telemetry and logging using TypeScript

import { TelemetryClient } from 'application-insights';

const telemetryClient = new TelemetryClient('instrumentationKey');

function trackError(error: Error): void {

telemetryClient.trackException({ exception: error });

}

function logEvent(eventName: string, properties?: { [key: string]: string }): void {

console.log(`Event: ${eventName}`);

if (properties) {

console.log('Properties:', properties);

}

}
```

In this example, TypeScript is used to define custom telemetry and logging functions using the Application Insights library.

Conclusion

TypeScript's strong

Section 14.2: Automating Builds and Deployments with TypeScript

Automating builds and deployments is a fundamental aspect of DevOps practices. In this section, we will explore how TypeScript can be used to automate these processes, making them more efficient and reliable.

Build Automation

Build automation involves the process of compiling, testing, and packaging an application for deployment. TypeScript's strong typing and tooling support make it well-suited for this purpose. Here are some ways TypeScript can be used for build automation:

1. **Task Runners**: TypeScript can be integrated with task runners like Gulp or Grunt to automate build tasks. You can define build scripts in TypeScript, ensuring that your build process is maintainable and efficient.

   // Example Gulpfile.js using TypeScript

   ```
   const gulp = require('gulp');

   const ts = require('gulp-typescript');

   const tsProject = ts.createProject('tsconfig.json');
   ```

```
gulp.task('build', function () {

return tsProject.src()

.pipe(tsProject())

.js.pipe(gulp.dest('dist'));

});
```

1. **Continuous Integration (CI)**: CI tools like Jenkins, Travis CI, or GitHub Actions can execute TypeScript build scripts automatically whenever changes are pushed to the repository. This ensures that your application is built consistently and any build errors are caught early.
2. **Dependency Management**: Tools like npm and yarn can be used to manage TypeScript dependencies and automate the installation of required packages during the build process.

Deployment Automation

Automating deployments is crucial for ensuring that applications are deployed consistently across different environments. TypeScript can be used to automate deployment scripts and workflows:

1. **Deployment Scripts**: TypeScript can be used to write deployment scripts that automate the process of deploying applications to various environments, such as development, staging, and production.

```
// Example deployment script using TypeScript

import { deployToDevelopment, deployToStaging,
deployToProduction } from './deployment-utils';
```

```typescript
const environment = process.env.DEPLOY_ENV ||
'development';

switch (environment) {

case 'staging':

deployToStaging();

break;

case 'production':

deployToProduction();

break;

default:

deployToDevelopment();

}
```

1. **Infrastructure as Code (IaC)**: TypeScript can be used to define infrastructure components and configurations using tools like AWS CDK, Terraform, or Azure Resource Manager templates. This allows you to automate the provisioning of infrastructure as part of your deployment process.

```typescript
// Example AWS CDK TypeScript code for defining AWS resources
import * as cdk from 'aws-cdk-lib';
```

```
import * as ec2 from 'aws-cdk-lib/aws-ec2';

const app = new cdk.App();

const stack = new cdk.Stack(app, 'MyStack');

const vpc = new ec2.Vpc(stack, 'MyVpc', {

maxAzs: 3,

subnetConfiguration: [

{

cidrMask: 24,

name: 'Public',

subnetType: ec2.SubnetType.PUBLIC,

},

],

});
```

1. **Containerization**: TypeScript can be used to automate the creation and deployment of containerized applications using Docker and Kubernetes. You can define Dockerfiles and Kubernetes YAML files in TypeScript, ensuring that containerized applications are consistent and reproducible.

// Example TypeScript code for defining a Kubernetes Deployment

```
import * as k8s from 'k8s';
```

```
const deployment = new k8s.apps.v1.Deployment('my-deployment', {

spec: {

replicas: 3,

template: {

metadata: { labels: { app: 'my-app' } },

spec: {

containers: [

{

name: 'my-container',

image: 'my-app:latest',

},

],

},

},

},

});
```

1. **Serverless Deployments**: For serverless architectures, TypeScript can be used to define serverless functions, APIs, and other resources in platforms like AWS Lambda, Azure Functions, or Google Cloud Functions. This allows for automated serverless deployments.

```
// Example AWS Lambda function definition using
TypeScript

import * as awsLambda from 'aws-lambda';

export const handler: awsLambda.Handler = async
(event, context) => {

// Lambda function logic here

};
```

Conclusion

Automating builds and deployments with TypeScript streamlines
the software delivery process, improves consistency, and reduces the
risk of errors. Whether you are working with traditional monolithic
applications or modern microservices architectures, TypeScript's
versatility and type safety can significantly enhance your DevOps
practices.

Section 14.3: TypeScript in Containerized Environments

Containerization has become a popular approach for packaging and
deploying applications consistently across different environments. In
this section, we will explore how TypeScript can be used effectively
in containerized environments, particularly with Docker and
Kubernetes.

Dockerizing TypeScript Applications

Docker is a containerization platform that allows you to package
applications and their dependencies into containers. TypeScript can
be used to create Dockerized applications efficiently:

- **Dockerfiles in TypeScript**: You can define Dockerfiles for your TypeScript applications. Dockerfiles are text files that specify the steps required to build a Docker image. TypeScript can be used to create Docker images, ensuring that your application's dependencies are properly configured.

```typescript
// Example Dockerfile in TypeScript

import { writeFileSync } from 'fs';

writeFileSync('Dockerfile', `

FROM node:14

WORKDIR /app

COPY package*.json ./

RUN npm install

COPY . .

EXPOSE 3000

CMD ["npm", "start"]

`);
```

- **Multi-stage Builds**: TypeScript can be used to implement multi-stage builds in Dockerfiles. This technique allows you to build and compile your TypeScript code in one stage and then create a smaller production-ready image in another stage. This reduces the size of the final Docker image.

```typescript
// Example multi-stage Dockerfile in TypeScript

import { writeFileSync } from 'fs';

writeFileSync('Dockerfile', `

# Stage 1: Build TypeScript code

FROM node:14 AS builder

WORKDIR /app

COPY package*.json ./

RUN npm install

COPY . .

RUN npm run build

# Stage 2: Create production-ready image

FROM node:14

WORKDIR /app

COPY—from=builder /app/dist ./dist

EXPOSE 3000

CMD ["node", "dist/main.js"]

`);
```

Kubernetes and TypeScript

Kubernetes is an open-source container orchestration platform that can manage containerized applications at scale. TypeScript can be used in conjunction with Kubernetes in the following ways:

- **Kubernetes API in TypeScript**: You can use TypeScript to interact with the Kubernetes API. Libraries like client-node provide TypeScript bindings for Kubernetes, allowing you to manage resources programmatically.

// Example TypeScript code for creating a Kubernetes Deployment

```typescript
import * as k8s from 'client-node';

const deployment = new k8s.apps.v1.Deployment('my-deployment', {

spec: {

replicas: 3,

template: {

metadata: { labels: { app: 'my-app' } },

spec: {

containers: [

{

name: 'my-container',
```

```
image: 'my-app:latest',

},

],

},

},

},

});
```

- **Helm Charts**: Helm is a package manager for Kubernetes that allows you to define, install, and upgrade even the most complex Kubernetes applications. Helm charts can be authored using TypeScript, making it easier to manage Kubernetes resources.

```
// Example TypeScript Helm chart definition

import { Chart } from 'cdk8s';

import { Deployment, Service } from 'cdk8s-plus';

export class MyChart extends Chart {

constructor(scope: Construct, id: string) {

super(scope, id);

// Define Kubernetes resources

const deployment = new Deployment(this, 'my-deployment', {
```

```
  replicas: 3,

  // ...

});

const service = new Service(this, 'my-service', {

  // ...

});

  }

}
```

Benefits of TypeScript in Containerized Environments

Using TypeScript in containerized environments offers several advantages:

- **Type Safety**: TypeScript provides strong typing, which helps catch errors at compile-time rather than runtime. This reduces the risk of misconfigurations in Dockerfiles, Kubernetes manifests, or Helm charts.

- **Improved Maintainability**: TypeScript's readability and maintainability make it easier to work with complex Dockerfiles and Kubernetes resources. Code auto-completion and type checking contribute to a smoother development experience.

- **Consistency**: TypeScript ensures that configurations and code for Docker and Kubernetes are consistent and well-structured. This consistency simplifies collaboration among team members.

- **Ecosystem Support**: TypeScript has a rich ecosystem of libraries and tools, which can be leveraged to simplify containerization and Kubernetes management tasks.

In conclusion, TypeScript can enhance the containerization and orchestration of applications in Docker and Kubernetes. Its strong typing, development productivity, and ecosystem support make it a valuable choice for managing containerized environments efficiently.

Section 14.4: Monitoring and Logging TypeScript Applications in Containers

Monitoring and logging are essential aspects of managing containerized applications, ensuring their reliability and performance. In this section, we'll explore how TypeScript can be used for effective monitoring and logging of applications running in containers.

Monitoring TypeScript Applications

Monitoring containerized TypeScript applications involves collecting and analyzing data about their performance, resource usage, and health. TypeScript's strong typing and modern tooling make it well-suited for implementing monitoring solutions. Here are some approaches:

- **Prometheus and TypeScript**: Prometheus is a popular open-source monitoring and alerting toolkit. You can use TypeScript to create custom exporters for Prometheus or instrument your TypeScript code with Prometheus client libraries to expose metrics.

```typescript
// Example TypeScript code for instrumenting with Prometheus

import * as promClient from 'prom-client';

const httpRequestDurationMicroseconds = new promClient.Histogram({

name: 'http_request_duration_seconds',

help: 'Duration of HTTP requests in seconds',

labelNames: ['route'],

});

// Middleware for measuring HTTP request duration
app.use((req, res, next) => {

const end = httpRequestDurationMicroseconds.startTimer();

res.on('finish', () => {

end({ route: req.route.path });

});

next();

});
```

- **Grafana and TypeScript**: Grafana is a popular open-source platform for monitoring and observability. You can use TypeScript to create custom data sources or panels for Grafana, allowing you to visualize and analyze metrics from your TypeScript applications.

```typescript
// Example TypeScript code for creating a custom Grafana panel

import { PanelPlugin } from '@grafana/ui';

export const myCustomPanel = new PanelPlugin<MyPanelOptions>(MyPanel);
```

Logging TypeScript Applications

Logging in containerized TypeScript applications is crucial for debugging and understanding their behavior. TypeScript provides excellent support for structured logging, making it easier to trace and analyze logs. Here are some approaches:

- **Winston and TypeScript**: Winston is a popular logging library for Node.js applications. You can use TypeScript with Winston to create structured logs with different log levels and formats.

```typescript
// Example TypeScript code for using Winston for logging

import * as winston from 'winston';

const logger = winston.createLogger({

level: 'info',

format: winston.format.json(),
```

```
transports: [

new winston.transports.Console(),

new winston.transports.File({ filename: 'error.log', level:
'error' }),

],

});

logger.info('This is an info log.');

logger.error('This is an error log.');
```

• **ELK Stack and TypeScript**: The ELK Stack (Elasticsearch, Logstash, Kibana) is a powerful solution for log management and analysis. TypeScript can be used to send structured logs to Logstash or Elasticsearch, making it easier to explore and visualize log data using Kibana.

```
// Example TypeScript code for sending logs to Logstash

import * as winston from 'winston';

import * as logstashTransport from 'winston-logstash-
transport';

const logger = winston.createLogger({

level: 'info',

format: winston.format.json(),
```

```
transports: [

new logstashTransport({

host: 'logstash-host',

port: 5044,

format: winston.format.json(),

}),

],

});

logger.info('This is an info log sent to Logstash.');
```

Benefits of TypeScript in Monitoring and Logging

Using TypeScript for monitoring and logging in containerized environments offers several advantages:

- **Type Safety**: TypeScript's strong typing ensures that log data and metrics are structured and consistent, reducing the risk of logging errors.

- **Tooling Support**: TypeScript benefits from a rich ecosystem of monitoring and logging libraries and tools, making it easy to integrate with existing solutions.

- **Development Productivity**: TypeScript's developer-friendly features, such as code completion and type checking, improve productivity when implementing monitoring and logging.

- **Consistency**: TypeScript promotes consistency in log and metric formats across different parts of your application, making it easier to correlate data.

In conclusion, TypeScript is a valuable choice for implementing monitoring and logging in containerized TypeScript applications. Its strong typing, development-friendly features, and compatibility with monitoring and logging tools make it well-suited for ensuring the reliability and performance of containerized applications.

Section 14.5: TypeScript in Microservice Orchestration

Microservices architecture has gained popularity due to its scalability, maintainability, and flexibility. TypeScript plays a significant role in microservice orchestration by enabling developers to build and manage microservices effectively. In this section, we will explore how TypeScript is used in microservices orchestration.

TypeScript and Microservices

Microservices are small, independently deployable services that work together to form an application. TypeScript's features, such as strong typing and modularity, make it well-suited for developing microservices. Here's how TypeScript benefits microservices:

- **Strong Typing**: TypeScript's static typing helps catch type-related errors at compile-time, reducing the chances of runtime errors in microservices.

- **Modularity**: TypeScript's support for modules and packages allows developers to create well-structured and maintainable microservices.

- **Tooling**: TypeScript's ecosystem includes tools like Nest.js and TypeScript Microservices Framework that simplify microservices development.

Communication between Microservices

In a microservices architecture, communication between services is critical. TypeScript provides several options for inter-service communication:

- **HTTP/REST**: TypeScript can be used to build microservices that communicate over HTTP using RESTful APIs. Libraries like Express.js make it easy to create HTTP-based microservices.

- **gRPC**: gRPC is a high-performance, language-agnostic RPC framework. TypeScript supports gRPC, allowing you to define service interfaces using Protocol Buffers and generate TypeScript code for clients and servers.

- **Message Queues**: TypeScript can be used with message queue systems like RabbitMQ or Kafka to implement asynchronous communication between microservices. Libraries like amqplib or node-rdkafka facilitate integration.

Microservices Orchestration Frameworks

Microservices often need orchestration to manage their lifecycle, scaling, and coordination. TypeScript-friendly frameworks provide essential features for orchestration:

- **Kubernetes**: Kubernetes is a popular container orchestration platform that supports TypeScript for defining custom resources, controllers, and operators.

- **Docker Compose**: TypeScript can be used to define multi-container applications using Docker Compose, making it easier to manage microservices in development environments.

TypeScript and Serverless Microservices

Serverless computing, such as AWS Lambda and Azure Functions, is another option for deploying microservices. TypeScript is well-suited for serverless development:

- **AWS Lambda**: TypeScript is a supported language for AWS Lambda, enabling developers to build serverless microservices.

- **Azure Functions**: TypeScript can be used with Azure Functions, allowing developers to write serverless microservices in a familiar language.

Challenges and Best Practices

While TypeScript offers many advantages in microservices development, there are challenges, such as managing service discovery, load balancing, and versioning. Best practices include using API gateways, service meshes, and centralized configuration management to address these challenges.

In conclusion, TypeScript is a valuable choice for developing microservices and orchestrating them in various deployment environments. Its strong typing, modularity, and compatibility with communication protocols and orchestration frameworks make it a powerful tool for building scalable and maintainable microservices architectures.

Chapter 15: TypeScript and the Cloud

Section 15.1: Cloud-native Development with TypeScript

In today's rapidly evolving tech landscape, cloud-native development has become a cornerstone for building scalable and resilient applications. TypeScript, with its statically typed nature and strong tooling support, is well-suited for cloud-native development. This section explores the synergy between TypeScript and cloud-native technologies, demonstrating how TypeScript can empower developers to create robust cloud-native applications.

Why TypeScript for Cloud-native Development?

Cloud-native development emphasizes microservices, serverless architectures, and containerization. TypeScript aligns seamlessly with these paradigms, offering advantages such as:

1. **Type Safety**: TypeScript's static typing helps catch errors early in the development process, reducing runtime issues in cloud-native applications.
2. **Tooling**: TypeScript benefits from excellent development tools and IDE support, enhancing developer productivity when working on cloud-native projects.
3. **Code Maintainability**: In a cloud-native environment with multiple microservices, maintaining code quality is crucial. TypeScript's strong typing and modularization features simplify code maintenance.

4. **Scalability**: As cloud-native applications need to scale effortlessly, TypeScript's ability to structure code into manageable modules is a significant advantage.

5. **TypeScript with JavaScript Ecosystem**: TypeScript interoperates seamlessly with JavaScript libraries and frameworks commonly used in cloud-native development, such as Node.js and Express.js.

TypeScript and Containerization

Containerization with technologies like Docker and Kubernetes is a common practice in cloud-native development. TypeScript plays a role in this context by enabling developers to build containerized applications efficiently. Developers can write TypeScript code that runs inside containers, providing consistency and predictability in a containerized environment.

Here's a basic example of a Dockerfile for a TypeScript application:

 # Use an official Node.js runtime as a parent image

FROM node:14

 # Set the working directory in the container

WORKDIR /usr/src/app

 # Copy package.json and package-lock.json to the container

COPY package*.json ./

 # Install application dependencies

RUN npm install

 # Copy the rest of the application code to the container

```
COPY ..

# Build the TypeScript code

RUN npm run build

# Expose a port for the application to listen on

EXPOSE 3000

# Define the command to run the application

CMD [ "npm", "start" ]
```

This Dockerfile sets up a Node.js environment, installs dependencies, builds the TypeScript code, exposes a port, and defines the command to start the application. It's a foundational piece for containerization, and TypeScript seamlessly fits into this workflow.

Serverless Architectures and TypeScript

Serverless computing, offered by platforms like AWS Lambda, Azure Functions, and Google Cloud Functions, is another key aspect of cloud-native development. TypeScript can be used to build serverless functions effectively. Developers can write TypeScript code and deploy it as serverless functions with minimal configuration.

Here's a simple TypeScript example of an AWS Lambda function:

```typescript
import { APIGatewayEvent, Context } from 'aws-lambda';

export const handler = async (

event: APIGatewayEvent,

context: Context
```

```typescript
): Promise<any> => {

try {

// Your serverless function logic here

return {

statusCode: 200,

body: JSON.stringify({ message: 'Hello from TypeScript Lambda!' }),

};

} catch (error) {

return {

statusCode: 500,

body: JSON.stringify({ error: 'Internal Server Error' }),

};

}

};
```

In this example, TypeScript provides type annotations for AWS Lambda event and context objects, making it easier to work with them. Serverless development becomes more efficient and reliable with TypeScript's help.

TypeScript and Cloud Databases

Cloud-native applications often require interaction with cloud databases like Amazon DynamoDB, Azure Cosmos DB, or Google

Cloud Firestore. TypeScript can enhance this interaction by providing type definitions for database models and queries. This ensures that database operations are type-safe and reduces the likelihood of runtime errors.

```typescript
import { DocumentClient } from 'aws-sdk/clients/dynamodb';

const dynamoDB = new DocumentClient();

// Define a TypeScript interface for a database item
interface TodoItem {

userId: string;

todoId: string;

createdAt: string;

name: string;

done: boolean;

}

// Example TypeScript function to fetch a todo item from DynamoDB

export async function getTodoItem(userId: string, todoId: string): Promise<TodoItem | undefined> {

const params = {

TableName: 'TodosTable',

Key: {

userId,

todoId,
```

```typescript
  },

};

const result = await dynamoDB.get(params).promise();

return result.Item as TodoItem;

}
```

In this example, TypeScript ensures that the getTodoItem function returns a well-defined TodoItem object or undefined, making it clear what consumers of this function can expect.

TypeScript and Cloud-native Best Practices

When developing cloud-native applications with TypeScript, it's essential to

Section 15.2: TypeScript with AWS, Azure, and Google Cloud

In cloud-native development, enterprises often rely on cloud providers like Amazon Web Services (AWS), Microsoft Azure, and Google Cloud Platform (GCP) for infrastructure and services. TypeScript seamlessly integrates with these cloud providers, enabling developers to harness the full power of their services while maintaining code quality and scalability.

TypeScript and AWS

AWS SDK and TypeScript

Amazon Web Services offers a comprehensive SDK that allows developers to interact with various AWS services programmatically. TypeScript can significantly enhance the development experience with AWS SDK by providing type definitions for AWS services and resources.

To work with AWS services in TypeScript, you typically install the AWS SDK for JavaScript and its associated type definitions:

npm install aws-sdk @types/aws-sdk—save

Once installed, you can use TypeScript to interact with AWS services, such as Amazon S3 for object storage, AWS Lambda for serverless computing, and Amazon DynamoDB for NoSQL database operations.

Here's an example of using TypeScript to interact with Amazon S3 to upload a file:

```typescript
import * as AWS from 'aws-sdk';

const s3 = new AWS.S3();

const uploadFile = async (bucketName: string, key: string, file: Buffer) => {

try {

const params = {

Bucket: bucketName,
```

```typescript
    Key: key,

    Body: file,

  };

  await s3.upload(params).promise();

  console.log(`File uploaded to ${bucketName}/${key}`);

  } catch (error) {

    console.error('Error uploading file:', error);

  }

};

// Usage

const myBucket = 'my-aws-bucket';

const myKey = 'example.txt';

const fileData = Buffer.from('Hello, AWS S3!');

uploadFile(myBucket, myKey, fileData);
```

In this TypeScript example, we use the AWS SDK to upload a file to an S3 bucket. TypeScript's type annotations provide clarity and safety during development.

AWS Lambda and TypeScript

AWS Lambda enables serverless computing, allowing you to run code in response to various events. TypeScript is a natural fit for developing Lambda functions due to its type safety and modularity.

Here's a TypeScript AWS Lambda function example:

```typescript
import { APIGatewayEvent, Context, Callback } from 'aws-lambda';

export const handler = async (

event: APIGatewayEvent,

context: Context,

callback: Callback

) => {

try {

// Lambda function logic here

const response = {

statusCode: 200,

body: JSON.stringify({ message: 'Hello from TypeScript Lambda!' }),

};

callback(null, response);

} catch (error) {

callback(error);

}

};
```

This example demonstrates the use of TypeScript in an AWS Lambda function that responds to API Gateway events. TypeScript ensures that event objects are properly typed, making development more reliable.

TypeScript and Azure

Azure SDK and TypeScript

Microsoft Azure offers an SDK that allows developers to interact with Azure services programmatically. TypeScript can enhance Azure development by providing type definitions for Azure services and resources.

To work with Azure services in TypeScript, you typically install the Azure SDK for JavaScript and its associated type definitions:

```
npm install @azure/storage-blob @types/azure-storage-blob —save
```

You can then use TypeScript to interact with Azure services like Azure Storage, Azure Functions, and Azure Cosmos DB.

Here's an example of using TypeScript to work with Azure Storage Blobs:

```
import { BlobServiceClient, ContainerClient, BlockBlobClient } from '@azure/storage-blob';

const connectionString = 'your-azure-storage-connection-string';

const containerName = 'my-container';

const blobServiceClient = BlobServiceClient.fromConnectionString(connectionString);

const containerClient = blobServiceClient.getContainerClient(containerName);
```

```typescript
const uploadBlob = async (fileName: string, data: Uint8Array) => {

const blockBlobClient = containerClient.getBlockBlobClient(fileName);

await blockBlobClient.upload(data, data.length);

console.log(`Blob "${fileName}" uploaded.`);

};

// Usage

const fileName = 'example.txt';

const fileData = Uint8Array.from(Buffer.from('Hello, Azure Blob Storage!'));

uploadBlob(fileName, fileData);
```

In this TypeScript example, we use the Azure SDK for JavaScript to upload a blob to an Azure Storage container. TypeScript ensures proper type annotations, helping prevent runtime errors.

Azure Functions and TypeScript

Azure Functions allow you to build serverless applications with event-driven architecture. TypeScript is a valuable tool for developing Azure Functions because it provides type safety and IDE support.

Here's an example of a TypeScript Azure Function:

```typescript
import { AzureFunction, Context, HttpRequest } from '@azure/functions';
```

```typescript
const httpTrigger: AzureFunction = async function (
context: Context,
req: HttpRequest
): Promise<void> {
context.log('HTTP trigger function processed a request.');
const name = (req.query.name || (req.body && req.body.name)) || 'Anonymous';
context.res = {
body: `Hello, ${name}!`,
};
};
export default httpTrigger;
```

In this example, TypeScript's type annotations for Azure

Section 15.3: Serverless Architectures and TypeScript

Serverless architecture has gained significant popularity in modern application development due to its scalability, cost-efficiency, and ease of management. TypeScript is a powerful language choice for developing serverless applications, as it brings type safety, enhanced tooling, and code maintainability to the serverless world.

TypeScript and AWS Lambda

Developing AWS Lambda Functions with TypeScript

AWS Lambda allows you to run code without provisioning or managing servers. TypeScript can be seamlessly integrated into AWS Lambda functions, providing benefits like:

- **Type Safety**: TypeScript's static typing helps identify and prevent errors at compile-time, reducing runtime issues in Lambda functions.

- **Code Clarity**: Type annotations make code more understandable, especially when dealing with event objects and data transformations.

- **Tooling Support**: TypeScript enjoys robust support from various Integrated Development Environments (IDEs) and code editors, enhancing the developer experience.

Here's a basic TypeScript example of an AWS Lambda function that handles an S3 event:

```typescript
import { S3Handler } from 'aws-lambda';

export const handler: S3Handler = async (event, context) => {

try {

const { Records } = event;

for (const record of Records) {

const { s3 } = record;
```

```typescript
const { bucket, object } = s3;

const { key } = object;

// Your Lambda function logic here

console.log(`File "${key}" in bucket "${bucket.name}" was created.`);

}

} catch (error) {

console.error('Error processing S3 event:', error);

}

};
```

In this example, TypeScript ensures that event objects are properly typed, making it easier to work with the event data. Any type mismatches or missing properties are caught at compile-time.

AWS CDK and TypeScript

The AWS Cloud Development Kit (CDK) is an infrastructure-as-code framework for defining cloud resources using familiar programming languages, including TypeScript. With the AWS CDK, you can define and provision AWS infrastructure and services programmatically.

Developing AWS CDK applications with TypeScript provides the following advantages:

- **Type Safety**: TypeScript brings type annotations to your CDK code, ensuring that your infrastructure definitions are correct and well-typed.

- **Code Reusability**: TypeScript's modularity allows you to create reusable constructs and patterns for your AWS resources.

- **IDE Support**: TypeScript benefits from excellent tooling support, including autocompletion, linting, and refactoring assistance.

Here's a TypeScript AWS CDK example that defines an Amazon S3 bucket:

```typescript
import { App, Stack, StackProps, Construct } from 'aws-cdk-lib';

import { Bucket } from 'aws-cdk-lib/aws-s3';

class MyS3Stack extends Stack {

constructor(scope: Construct, id: string, props?: StackProps) {

super(scope, id, props);

// Create an S3 bucket

new Bucket(this, 'MyS3Bucket', {

versioned: true,

});

}

}

const app = new App();
```

```
new MyS3Stack(app, 'MyS3Stack');
```

In this TypeScript CDK code, we define an Amazon S3 bucket with versioning enabled. TypeScript's type system ensures that our CDK constructs are correctly configured.

TypeScript and Azure Functions

Developing Azure Functions with TypeScript

Azure Functions allow you to build serverless applications with event-driven architecture. TypeScript enhances the development experience by providing type safety, code clarity, and IDE support.

Here's an example of a TypeScript Azure Function:

```typescript
import { AzureFunction, Context, HttpRequest } from '@azure/functions';

const httpTrigger: AzureFunction = async function (
context: Context,
req: HttpRequest
): Promise<void> {
context.log('HTTP trigger function processed a request.');
const name = (req.query.name || (req.body && req.body.name)) || 'Anonymous';
context.res = {
body: `Hello, ${name}!`,
};
```

```
};
```

export default httpTrigger;

In this TypeScript Azure Function, type annotations clarify the structure of the function, making it easier to understand and maintain. TypeScript also offers intellisense and type checking, reducing the likelihood of errors.

Azure Durable Functions and TypeScript

Azure Durable Functions allow you to write stateful serverless workflows using Azure Functions. TypeScript can help ensure the correctness and reliability of your durable workflows.

Here's an example of a TypeScript Azure Durable Function that implements a simple approval workflow:

```
import { DurableOrchestrationContext, IOrchestrationFunctionContext } from 'azure-functions-ts-essentials';

const approvalWorkflow = async (

context: DurableOrchestrationContext

): Promise<string> => {

const input = context.df.getInput();

// Implement your approval logic here (e.g., send notifications, wait for responses)

const approvalResult = 'Approved'; // Replace with the actual approval result
```

return approvalResult;

};

export default approvalWorkflow;

In this TypeScript Durable Function, TypeScript's type annotations help define the function's input and output types, ensuring that the workflow behaves as expected.

TypeScript and Google Cloud Functions

Developing Google Cloud Functions with TypeScript

Google

Section 15.4: Building and Deploying Cloud Functions with TypeScript

Developing cloud functions is a common practice in cloud-native development for building small, focused pieces of code that respond to events or triggers. TypeScript is well-suited for building and deploying cloud functions across different cloud providers, including AWS Lambda, Azure Functions, and Google Cloud Functions. In this section, we'll explore how to create, build, and deploy cloud functions using TypeScript.

Setting Up Your Development Environment

Before you start building cloud functions with TypeScript, ensure that you have a proper development environment set up. You'll need Node.js and npm installed on your machine. You can create a new TypeScript project using tools like npm, yarn, or npx. Here's an example of how to set up a new TypeScript project using npm:

 # Create a new directory for your project

mkdir my-cloud-functions

 # Navigate to the project directory

cd my-cloud-functions

 # Initialize a new Node.js project

npm init -y

 # Install TypeScript and TypeScript Compiler (tsc)

npm install typescript ts-node—save-dev

 # Initialize a TypeScript configuration file

npx tsc—init

Now you have a basic TypeScript project set up and ready for building cloud functions.

Creating a Cloud Function

To create a cloud function with TypeScript, you can create a new TypeScript file (e.g., my-function.ts) and define your function. Below is a simple example of a TypeScript cloud function using the AWS Lambda event handler:

```typescript
import { APIGatewayEvent, Context, Callback } from 'aws-lambda';

export const handler = async (
event: APIGatewayEvent,
context: Context,
callback: Callback
```

```typescript
) => {
try {
// Your cloud function logic here
const response = {
statusCode: 200,
body: JSON.stringify({ message: 'Hello from TypeScript Lambda!' }),
};
callback(null, response);
} catch (error) {
callback(error);
}
};
```

In this example, the handler function is an AWS Lambda function that responds to API Gateway events. TypeScript provides type annotations for event objects and ensures type safety throughout your code.

Compiling TypeScript to JavaScript

Before deploying your TypeScript cloud function, you need to compile it to JavaScript. TypeScript comes with a command-line compiler, tsc, which can transpile your TypeScript code to JavaScript. To compile your TypeScript code, run the following command in your project directory:

npx tsc

This command will create a dist folder containing the compiled JavaScript files, which you can deploy to your cloud provider.

Deploying to AWS Lambda

To deploy your TypeScript cloud function to AWS Lambda, you can use AWS's Serverless Application Model (SAM) or frameworks like Serverless Framework or AWS CDK. Here's an example of deploying a TypeScript function using the Serverless Framework:

1. Install the Serverless Framework globally if you haven't already:

npm install -g serverless

1. Create a serverless.yml file in your project directory with the following configuration:

service: my-cloud-functions

provider:

name: aws

runtime: nodejs14.x

functions:

myFunction:

handler: dist/my-function.handler

1. Deploy your function to AWS Lambda using Serverless Framework:

serverless deploy

This command will package and deploy your TypeScript function to AWS Lambda.

Deploying to Azure Functions

To deploy your TypeScript cloud function to Azure Functions, you can use Azure Functions Core Tools or Azure DevOps CI/CD pipelines. Here's an example of deploying a TypeScript function using Azure Functions Core Tools:

1. Install Azure Functions Core Tools if you haven't already:

npm install -g azure-functions-core-tools@3—unsafe-perm true

1. Create a local.settings.json file in your project directory with the following configuration:

{

"IsEncrypted": **false**,

"Values": {

"AzureWebJobsStorage": "UseDevelopmentStorage=true"

}

}

1. Deploy your function to Azure Functions:

func azure functionapp publish my-azure-function-app

Replace my-azure-function-app with the name of your Azure Function App.

Deploying to Google Cloud Functions

To deploy your TypeScript cloud function to Google Cloud Functions, you can use the gcloud command-line tool or Google Cloud Build. Here's an example of deploying a TypeScript function using gcloud:

1. Install the gcloud command-line tool if you haven't already and configure it with your Google Cloud credentials.
2. Deploy your function to Google Cloud Functions:

gcloud functions deploy my-function \

—runtime nodejs14 \

—trigger-http \

—allow-unauthenticated \

—entry-point handler \

—source dist

Replace my-function with the name of your Google Cloud Function.

Testing Your Cloud Function Locally

Before deploying your TypeScript cloud function, it's a good practice to test it locally to ensure it works as expected. You can use the local development tools provided by your cloud provider or tools like the serverless offline plugin for AWS Lambda or the Azure Functions Core Tools for Azure Functions.

Monitoring and Debugging

Once your TypeScript cloud function is deployed, you'll want to monitor its performance and handle any errors that may occur in the cloud environment. Cloud providers offer monitoring and logging services that you can integrate with your functions to gain insights into their behavior.

Additionally, you can use debugging tools provided by your cloud provider or third-party debugging tools to troubleshoot issues in your TypeScript cloud functions.

In conclusion, TypeScript is a valuable choice for building and deploying cloud functions in a cloud-native development environment. Its type safety, code clarity, and tooling support make it easier to develop, maintain, and deploy serverless code across various cloud providers. Whether you're using AWS Lambda, Azure Functions, Google Cloud Functions, or other serverless platforms, TypeScript can streamline your development process and help you create reliable and scalable cloud functions.

Section 15.5: Managing Cloud Resources with TypeScript

Managing cloud resources is an essential aspect of cloud-native development. Whether you're using AWS, Azure, Google Cloud, or any other cloud provider, TypeScript can be a valuable tool for automating and managing your cloud infrastructure. In this section, we'll explore how TypeScript can be used to manage and provision cloud resources effectively.

Infrastructure as Code (IaC)

Infrastructure as Code (IaC) is an approach that involves managing and provisioning cloud resources using code rather than manual processes. With IaC, you can define your infrastructure, including virtual machines, databases, storage, and networking, in a declarative manner. TypeScript, when combined with cloud-specific SDKs and libraries, enables you to create and manage IaC scripts effectively.

Using TypeScript for IaC

To get started with managing cloud resources using TypeScript, you'll need to use the SDKs or libraries provided by your chosen cloud provider. Each cloud provider, such as AWS, Azure, and Google Cloud, offers TypeScript SDKs that allow you to interact with their services programmatically.

Here's a high-level overview of how you can use TypeScript for managing cloud resources:

1. **Install and Configure the Cloud SDK**: Begin by installing the cloud provider's SDK for TypeScript using npm or yarn. Configure the SDK with your credentials and authentication details.
2. **Create TypeScript Scripts**: Write TypeScript scripts to define and provision your cloud resources. These scripts can include resource definitions, configuration settings, and any logic required for resource creation.
3. **Use TypeScript SDK Functions**: Utilize the functions and classes provided by the cloud provider's TypeScript SDK to interact with their services. For example, you can create virtual machines, configure storage, set up databases, and manage networking resources.
4. **Manage Resource Lifecycle**: TypeScript allows you to not

only create resources but also manage their lifecycle. You can update, delete, and scale resources as needed by modifying your TypeScript code.

5. **Infrastructure Orchestration**: You can orchestrate complex cloud infrastructures by writing TypeScript code that creates and connects various resources. This can include provisioning resources in response to events or based on application requirements.

6. **Testing and Validation**: Before applying your TypeScript scripts to your cloud environment, it's crucial to test and validate them locally using cloud development emulators or mock libraries provided by the cloud provider. This ensures that your scripts work as expected.

Example: Creating an AWS S3 Bucket with TypeScript

Here's a simple example of how to use TypeScript to create an AWS S3 bucket using the AWS SDK for TypeScript:

```typescript
import { S3 } from 'aws-sdk';

// Initialize the AWS S3 client

const s3 = new S3();

// Define the S3 bucket parameters

const bucketName = 'my-unique-bucket-name';

// Create an S3 bucket

s3.createBucket({ Bucket: bucketName }, (err, data) => {
  if (err) {
```

```
console.error('Error creating S3 bucket:', err);

} else {

console.log('S3 bucket created successfully:', data.Location);

}

});
```

In this example, we import the AWS SDK for TypeScript, initialize an S3 client, and then use the createBucket function to create an S3 bucket with the specified name.

Infrastructure as Code Tools

While writing TypeScript code to manage cloud resources is powerful, many developers prefer to use Infrastructure as Code (IaC) tools that abstract away the underlying cloud-specific code. Tools like AWS CloudFormation, Azure Resource Manager (ARM) templates, and Terraform provide a higher-level, declarative approach to defining cloud infrastructure. These tools support TypeScript and other programming languages, allowing you to manage resources more efficiently.

By integrating TypeScript with IaC tools, you can enjoy the benefits of both code-based resource management and infrastructure orchestration, making your cloud resource management more streamlined and maintainable.

Conclusion

Using TypeScript for managing cloud resources brings several advantages to cloud-native development. TypeScript's strong typing, code clarity, and tooling support can enhance the way you define, provision, and manage cloud resources. Whether you choose to write custom TypeScript scripts for resource management or leverage Infrastructure as Code tools that support TypeScript, this approach can help you automate and maintain your cloud infrastructure more effectively, ensuring reliability and scalability in your cloud-native applications.

Chapter 16: TypeScript for Game Development

Game development is a dynamic and exciting field that often demands a blend of creativity and technical expertise. TypeScript has been gaining popularity as a language choice for game development due to its advantages in terms of type safety, tooling, and maintainability. In this chapter, we'll explore how TypeScript can be used in various aspects of game development, from setting up your development environment to creating interactive games with WebGL and physics libraries.

Section 16.1: Setting Up a Game Development Environment with TypeScript

Before diving into game development with TypeScript, it's essential to set up a suitable development environment. This environment includes the necessary tools, libraries, and configurations to streamline your game development process. In this section, we'll discuss the steps to set up a game development environment with TypeScript.

Choosing a Game Engine

One of the first decisions you'll need to make is whether to build your game engine from scratch or use an existing game engine. Building a game engine from scratch can be a daunting task, often requiring extensive low-level programming knowledge. On the other hand, using an existing game engine can significantly speed up development.

Popular game engines that support TypeScript or JavaScript include **Phaser**, **Babylon.js**, and **Three.js**. These engines provide a wide range of features, such as rendering, physics, and input handling, allowing you to focus on creating the game's content.

Setting Up a Development Environment

To set up a game development environment with TypeScript, follow these steps:

1. **Install Node.js**: Ensure that you have Node.js installed on your system. Node.js is essential for running TypeScript and various development tools.
2. **Initialize a TypeScript Project**: Create a new directory for your game project and run npm init to initialize a new Node.js project. Follow the prompts to set up your package.json file.
3. **Install TypeScript**: Install TypeScript globally using npm install -g typescript, or install it locally as a development dependency with npm install typescript—save-dev. It's a good practice to have TypeScript as a project dependency.
4. **Configure TypeScript**: Create a tsconfig.json file in your project directory to configure TypeScript. You can set options such as target ECMAScript version, module system, and output directory. For example:

```
{

"compilerOptions": {

"target": "ES6",

"module": "ESNext",

"outDir": "./dist"
```

```
    }

    }
```

1. **Install Development Tools**: Depending on your chosen game engine and development workflow, you may need additional development tools and libraries. For instance, if you're using Phaser, you can install it using npm install phaser.

2. **Code Editor**: Choose a code editor or integrated development environment (IDE) that supports TypeScript. Popular options include Visual Studio Code, WebStorm, and Atom. Install any necessary extensions or plugins for TypeScript support.

Creating Your First Game

With your development environment set up, you can start creating your first game. Here's a basic example of a Phaser game in TypeScript:

```typescript
import 'phaser';

const config: Phaser.Types.Core.GameConfig = {

type: Phaser.AUTO,

width: 800,

height: 600,

scene: {

preload: preload,

create: create,
```

```typescript
},

};

const game = new Phaser.Game(config);

function preload() {

// Load game assets here

}

function create() {

// Create game objects and set up gameplay here

}
```

This code sets up a Phaser game with TypeScript. You'll need to add your game's assets and logic within the preload and create functions.

Conclusion

Setting up a game development environment with TypeScript is the first step towards creating interactive and engaging games. By choosing the right game engine, configuring TypeScript, and using a suitable code editor, you can streamline your development process and focus on bringing your game ideas to life. In the following sections of this chapter, we'll delve deeper into various aspects of game development with TypeScript, including graphics rendering, physics simulation, and multiplayer game development.

Section 16.2: TypeScript in Canvas and WebGL

Canvas and WebGL are powerful technologies that enable rendering graphics and animations directly in web browsers. They are essential for building 2D and 3D games in web development. In this section, we'll explore how TypeScript can be used to harness the capabilities of Canvas and WebGL for game development.

HTML5 Canvas and TypeScript

HTML5 Canvas is a versatile technology that allows you to draw 2D graphics, images, and animations directly on a web page. TypeScript provides a robust way to work with Canvas, offering type safety and better code organization.

To get started with Canvas in TypeScript, you can create a Canvas element in your HTML file and then interact with it using TypeScript. Here's a simple example:

```typescript
const canvas = document.getElementById('game-canvas') as HTMLCanvasElement;

const ctx = canvas.getContext('2d');

if (ctx) {

// Drawing code here

}
```

In this code, we obtain a reference to the Canvas element and its 2D rendering context. With TypeScript, you can benefit from autocompletion and type checking while working with Canvas APIs, making it easier to create interactive graphics.

WebGL and TypeScript

WebGL, or Web Graphics Library, is a JavaScript API for rendering 3D graphics within web browsers. It leverages the power of the GPU to achieve high-performance graphics rendering. TypeScript is an excellent choice for WebGL development due to its type safety and advanced tooling.

Here's a basic example of setting up a WebGL context in TypeScript:

```typescript
const canvas = document.getElementById('game-canvas') as HTMLCanvasElement;

const gl = canvas.getContext('webgl');

if (!gl) {

console.error('WebGL not supported');

} else {

// WebGL initialization and rendering code here

}
```

WebGL development often involves shader programming, which requires precise data types and memory management. TypeScript's type system can help catch errors early in the development process, reducing debugging efforts.

Game Development with Canvas and WebGL

When building games with Canvas and WebGL in TypeScript, you'll need to handle tasks such as rendering game objects, managing animations, and handling user input. Frameworks like Phaser, Babylon.js, and Three.js provide TypeScript support and simplify these tasks.

Here's a simple example of rendering a rotating cube using Three.js and TypeScript:

```typescript
import * as THREE from 'three';

const scene = new THREE.Scene();

const camera = new THREE.PerspectiveCamera(75,
window.innerWidth / window.innerHeight, 0.1, 1000);

const renderer = new THREE.WebGLRenderer();

renderer.setSize(window.innerWidth, window.innerHeight);

document.body.appendChild(renderer.domElement);

const geometry = new THREE.BoxGeometry();

const material = new THREE.MeshBasicMaterial({ color: 0x00ff00
});

const cube = new THREE.Mesh(geometry, material);

scene.add(cube);

camera.position.z = 5;

const animate = () => {

requestAnimationFrame(animate);

cube.rotation.x += 0.01;

cube.rotation.y += 0.01;

renderer.render(scene, camera);

};
```

animate();

This code uses Three.js to create a rotating cube in a TypeScript project. It demonstrates how TypeScript can be used to work with WebGL and create interactive 3D graphics.

Conclusion

Canvas and WebGL are essential technologies for game development in web browsers, and TypeScript enhances the development experience by providing type safety and better code organization. Whether you're creating 2D games with Canvas or diving into 3D graphics with WebGL, TypeScript can help you build robust and interactive games for the web. In the next sections, we'll explore more advanced topics in game development with TypeScript, including integrating physics and animation libraries and developing multiplayer games.

Section 16.3: Integrating Physics and Animation Libraries

Integrating physics and animation libraries is crucial for creating dynamic and engaging games in TypeScript. These libraries help you simulate real-world physics, handle animations, and make your game characters and objects come to life. In this section, we'll explore how TypeScript can be used to integrate physics and animation libraries into your game development projects.

Physics Engines and TypeScript

Physics engines are essential for simulating realistic physical interactions in games. Libraries like Cannon.js and Ammo.js provide physics simulation capabilities that can be integrated into TypeScript projects seamlessly.

Here's an example of setting up a simple physics scene using Cannon.js and TypeScript:

```typescript
import * as CANNON from 'cannon';

// Create a world

const world = new CANNON.World();

world.gravity.set(0, -9.82, 0); // Set gravity

// Create a ground plane

const groundShape = new CANNON.Plane();

const groundBody = new CANNON.Body({ mass: 0 });

groundBody.addShape(groundShape);

world.addBody(groundBody);

// Create a dynamic sphere

const sphereShape = new CANNON.Sphere(1);

const sphereBody = new CANNON.Body({ mass: 1 });

sphereBody.addShape(sphereShape);

sphereBody.position.set(0, 10, 0);

world.addBody(sphereBody);

// Simulation loop

function animate() {

requestAnimationFrame(animate);

// Step the physics simulation
```

```
world.step(1 / 60);
```

```
// Update graphics here based on physics data
```

```
}
```

```
animate();
```

In this code, we create a basic physics scene with a ground plane and a dynamic sphere using Cannon.js. TypeScript's type checking helps ensure that physics-related code is correctly structured and free of errors.

Animation Libraries and TypeScript

Animation libraries like GreenSock Animation Platform (GSAP) and Three.js Animation system can be used to create smooth animations for game characters and objects. TypeScript's strong typing and autocompletion make it easier to work with animation-related code.

Here's an example of using GSAP for animation in TypeScript:

```
import gsap from 'gsap';
```

```
const character = document.getElementById('game-character');
```

```
gsap.to(character, { x: 200, duration: 2, ease: 'power2.out' });
```

In this code, we use GSAP to animate a game character's movement. TypeScript allows us to define animation parameters with confidence, reducing the likelihood of runtime errors.

Combining Physics and Animation

Integrating physics and animation libraries can lead to exciting gameplay experiences. For example, you can use physics simulations to model character movements and interactions with the environment, while animation libraries handle visual effects and character animations.

Here's a simplified example of combining Cannon.js physics and GSAP animation in TypeScript:

```typescript
// Initialize physics and animation

const world = new CANNON.World();

// ...

const character = document.getElementById('game-character');

// Animation loop

function animate() {

requestAnimationFrame(animate);

// Step the physics simulation

world.step(1 / 60);

// Update character's position based on physics

character.style.transform                                        =
`translateX(${sphereBody.position.x}px)
translateY(${sphereBody.position.y}px)`;

// Perform animations using GSAP

gsap.to(character, { rotation: '+=360', duration: 1 });

// Additional animation and game logic here

}
```

animate();

In this example, the physics simulation from Cannon.js is used to control the character's position, while GSAP handles the character's rotation animation. TypeScript ensures that the integration between physics and animation is seamless and error-free.

Conclusion

Integrating physics and animation libraries is essential for creating dynamic and visually appealing games. TypeScript's type safety and advanced tooling make it easier to work with these libraries and ensure that your game's physics and animations behave as expected. In the next section, we'll delve into the development of multiplayer games using TypeScript, exploring concepts like real-time networking and synchronization.

Section 16.4: TypeScript in Multiplayer Game Development

Multiplayer games are a popular genre in the world of video games, and TypeScript can play a significant role in their development. Creating a multiplayer game involves handling real-time communication, synchronization, and ensuring a fair and enjoyable experience for all players. In this section, we'll explore how TypeScript can be utilized in multiplayer game development.

Real-Time Networking

One of the key aspects of multiplayer game development is real-time networking. TypeScript can be used to implement networking solutions that allow players to interact with each other in real time. Libraries like socket.io provide an excellent foundation for building multiplayer games.

Here's an example of setting up a basic server and client using socket.io with TypeScript:

Server (Node.js):

```typescript
import { Server, Socket } from 'socket.io';

const io = new Server();

io.on('connection', (socket: Socket) => {

console.log(`Player ${socket.id} connected`);

socket.on('move', (data) => {

// Handle player movement

// Broadcast the updated player position to other players

socket.broadcast.emit('playerMoved', data);

});

socket.on('disconnect', () => {

console.log(`Player ${socket.id} disconnected`);

});

});

io.listen(3000);
```

Client (Browser):

```typescript
import { io } from 'socket.io-client';

const socket = io('http://localhost:3000');

// Listen for player movement updates from the server
```

```
socket.on('playerMoved', (data) => {

// Update the game world with the new player position

});
```

In this example, TypeScript helps ensure that the server and client code is type-safe, reducing the chances of runtime errors during real-time communication.

Synchronization and Fairness

Multiplayer games require careful synchronization to ensure that all players have a consistent view of the game world. TypeScript's type checking can assist in managing the game state and ensuring fairness.

For example, TypeScript can be used to define the game state and validate player actions:

```
type GameState = {

players: Player[];

obstacles: Obstacle[];

// ...other game data

};

type PlayerAction = {

type: 'move';

playerId: string;

newPosition: Position;

};
```

```
function applyPlayerAction(gameState: GameState, action:
PlayerAction) {

// Validate the action and update the game state

// Ensure that the action is valid based on game rules

}
```

By defining clear types and validation logic, TypeScript helps prevent cheating and ensures that all players have a fair and consistent gaming experience.

Scalability and Deployment

Multiplayer games often need to handle a large number of concurrent players. TypeScript's scalability and support for asynchronous programming can be beneficial when building server infrastructure to accommodate a growing player base. Tools like Docker and Kubernetes can be used to deploy TypeScript-based game servers at scale.

Conclusion

Multiplayer game development is a complex but rewarding endeavor, and TypeScript's strong typing, real-time networking capabilities, and support for scalability make it a valuable tool for creating engaging and fair multiplayer gaming experiences. In the next section, we'll explore managing dependencies and optimizing performance in large TypeScript projects.

Section 16.5: Case Studies: TypeScript in Popular Games

In this section, we'll take a look at case studies of how TypeScript has been used in popular games. TypeScript's combination of strong typing, modern language features, and tooling has made it an attractive choice for game developers looking to improve code quality, maintainability, and productivity.

1. *Hollow Knight: Silksong*

Hollow Knight: Silksong

Hollow Knight: Silksong is an eagerly anticipated sequel to the critically acclaimed indie game *Hollow Knight*. Team Cherry, the game's developer, adopted TypeScript for the development of both games. TypeScript's type system helped catch bugs early in development and provided better tooling for refactoring and managing complex game logic.

The developers praised TypeScript for its ability to scale with their projects as they expanded their game world and added new features. It allowed them to write cleaner, more maintainable code, ultimately contributing to the success of their games.

2. *Phaser 3*

Phaser 3

Phaser 3 is a popular open-source game framework used by game developers to create 2D games for the web. While the framework itself is written in JavaScript, many developers use TypeScript to build their games on top of Phaser 3.

TypeScript provides enhanced code completion and error checking when working with the Phaser 3 framework, making it easier to create complex games. The type definitions for Phaser 3 allow developers to benefit from strong typing while utilizing a powerful game development framework.

3. *Dead Cells*

Dead Cells

Dead Cells is a roguelike metroidvania action-platformer developed by Motion Twin. The game, praised for its tight controls and challenging gameplay, was partially written in TypeScript.

TypeScript helped the development team maintain a large and complex codebase, ensuring that changes and additions to the game didn't introduce subtle bugs. It also aided in managing dependencies and improving the overall stability of the game.

4. *Ori and the Will of the Wisps*

Ori and the Will of the Wisps

Ori and the Will of the Wisps, a visually stunning platformer developed by Moon Studios, also utilized TypeScript. The game's intricate animations, physics, and mechanics were made more manageable with TypeScript's static typing and IDE support.

TypeScript allowed Moon Studios to work efficiently on a game with highly polished visuals and intricate gameplay mechanics. It helped maintain a robust and reliable codebase for an exceptional gaming experience.

5. *Minecraft Dungeons*

Minecraft Dungeons

Minecraft Dungeons, a dungeon-crawling action-adventure game set in the *Minecraft* universe, incorporated TypeScript into its development. The game features real-time combat, procedurally generated levels, and a wide variety of character abilities.

TypeScript's static analysis capabilities were especially valuable in ensuring the reliability of game mechanics and balancing character abilities. It helped the development team maintain consistency and quality throughout the project.

These case studies demonstrate the versatility of TypeScript in the gaming industry. Whether used in indie titles or larger-scale projects, TypeScript has proven to be a valuable tool for game developers, enabling them to create polished, bug-free games while maintaining productivity and code quality.

Chapter 17: Security Practices in TypeScript

Section 17.1: Security Best Practices in TypeScript Development

Security is a critical aspect of software development, and TypeScript offers several features and best practices that can help developers create more secure applications. In this section, we will explore some essential security best practices when using TypeScript for application development.

1. Input Validation and Sanitization

One of the fundamental principles of security is to validate and sanitize user inputs. TypeScript encourages strong typing, making it easier to define strict input and output types. By enforcing input validation at the type level, you can reduce the risk of injection attacks such as SQL injection or cross-site scripting (XSS). Additionally, you should use libraries like DOMPurify for sanitizing user-generated HTML content to prevent XSS attacks in web applications.

```
// Input validation for user input

function processUserInput(input: string): void {

if (/^[a-zA-Z]+$/.test(input)) {

// Valid input

// ...

} else {
```

```
// Invalid input

// ...

}

}
```

2. Avoiding Hardcoded Secrets

Storing sensitive information, such as API keys or passwords, directly in your TypeScript source code is a security risk. Instead, utilize environment variables or configuration files to store and access such secrets. Tools like dotenv can help manage environment variables easily.

```
// Loading secrets from environment variables

const apiKey = process.env.API_KEY;

const dbPassword = process.env.DB_PASSWORD;
```

3. Authentication and Authorization

Implement strong authentication and authorization mechanisms in your applications. TypeScript's strong typing can be leveraged to define roles and permissions effectively. Consider using libraries like Passport.js for authentication and role-based access control (RBAC) for authorization.

```
// Role-based access control (RBAC)

enum UserRole {

User = 'user',

Admin = 'admin',
```

```typescript
}

function checkPermission(userRole: UserRole, requiredRole:
UserRole): boolean {

return userRole === requiredRole;

}
```

4. Error Handling

Proper error handling is crucial for security. Avoid exposing sensitive information in error messages sent to clients. Use custom error classes to handle different types of errors gracefully and securely.

```typescript
// Custom error class

class AppError extends Error {

constructor(message: string, public status: number) {

super(message);

this.name = this.constructor.name;

Error.captureStackTrace(this, this.constructor);

}

}
```

5. Security Libraries and Tools

Leverage security libraries and tools specifically designed for TypeScript and JavaScript development. For example, libraries like helmet can help secure Express.js applications by setting various HTTP headers to prevent common web vulnerabilities.

// Using the Helmet middleware in an Express.js app

```typescript
import express from 'express';

import helmet from 'helmet';

const app = express();

app.use(helmet());
```

6. Regular Security Audits

Regularly conduct security audits and code reviews to identify and fix security vulnerabilities in your TypeScript codebase. Utilize security scanning tools like OWASP ZAP and eslint-plugin-security to automate some aspects of security checks.

 # Running security audits with OWASP ZAP

```
zap-cli quick-scan—self-contained http://localhost:3000
```

By following these security best practices and staying informed about the latest security threats and updates, TypeScript developers can significantly improve the security posture of their applications and protect them from potential vulnerabilities and attacks.

Section 17.2: Handling Sensitive Data in TypeScript Applications

Handling sensitive data, such as personal information or payment details, in TypeScript applications requires a high level of care and security. In this section, we'll discuss best practices for managing sensitive data to ensure the confidentiality and integrity of this information.

1. Data Encryption

Encrypting sensitive data both at rest and in transit is a fundamental security measure. TypeScript applications can leverage encryption libraries like crypto to encrypt and decrypt data. Use industry-standard encryption algorithms and practices to protect sensitive data from unauthorized access.

```typescript
import crypto from 'crypto';

// Encrypting data

function encryptData(data: string, key: string): string {

const cipher = crypto.createCipher('aes-256-cbc', key);

let encrypted = cipher.update(data, 'utf8', 'hex');

encrypted += cipher.final('hex');

return encrypted;

}
```

2. Password Hashing

When storing user passwords, avoid saving them in plain text. Instead, use a secure password hashing library like bcrypt to hash and verify passwords. This ensures that even if the database is compromised, the passwords remain protected.

```typescript
import bcrypt from 'bcrypt';

// Hashing a password

async function hashPassword(password: string): Promise<string> {

const saltRounds = 10;
```

```typescript
const hash = await bcrypt.hash(password, saltRounds);

return hash;

}

// Verifying a password

async function verifyPassword(password: string, hash: string): Promise<boolean> {

return bcrypt.compare(password, hash);

}
```

3. Secure Storage

When storing sensitive data, choose storage solutions that provide robust security mechanisms. For example, if you're working with databases, use database encryption and access controls to protect the data. Additionally, implement proper access controls in your TypeScript application to restrict access to sensitive data based on user roles and permissions.

```typescript
// Sample access control middleware

function restrictToAdmin(req, res, next) {

if (req.user && req.user.role === 'admin') {

next();

} else {

res.status(403).send('Access denied');

}
```

```
}
```

4. API Security

When designing APIs that handle sensitive data, implement proper authentication and authorization mechanisms. Use technologies like OAuth 2.0 or JSON Web Tokens (JWT) to secure API endpoints. Ensure that API endpoints are properly validated and sanitized to prevent injection attacks.

```typescript
// Using JWT for authentication

import jwt from 'jsonwebtoken';

const secretKey = 'your-secret-key';

function generateToken(userId: string): string {

const token = jwt.sign({ userId }, secretKey, { expiresIn: '1h' });

return token;

}
```

5. Regular Security Audits

Perform regular security audits and penetration testing to identify vulnerabilities in your TypeScript application. Tools like OWASP ZAP and Nessus can help assess your application's security posture. Address any vulnerabilities promptly and keep your dependencies up to date to mitigate security risks.

```
# Running Nessus security scans

nessuscli scan—host your-app-url—policy security-audit-policy
```

6. Compliance with Data Protection Regulations

If your application handles sensitive user data, ensure compliance with data protection regulations such as GDPR, HIPAA, or CCPA. Implement features like data access requests and data deletion requests to fulfill legal requirements and protect user privacy.

By following these best practices, TypeScript developers can build applications that handle sensitive data securely, reducing the risk of data breaches and ensuring the trust and privacy of users. Always stay updated with the latest security threats and practices to continuously improve the security of your TypeScript applications.

Section 17.3: TypeScript for Secure Backend Development

Developing a secure backend in TypeScript is crucial to protect sensitive data and prevent unauthorized access to your application's resources. In this section, we'll explore key considerations and best practices for building a secure TypeScript backend.

1. Authentication and Authorization

Authentication verifies the identity of users or services accessing your backend, while authorization determines what actions they are allowed to perform. Implement strong authentication mechanisms, such as OAuth, JWT, or API keys, and use role-based access control (RBAC) to manage permissions effectively.

```typescript
// Middleware for authentication using JWT

import jwt from 'jsonwebtoken';

const secretKey = 'your-secret-key';
```

```javascript
function authenticate(req, res, next) {

const token = req.headers.authorization?.split(' ')[1];

if (!token) {

return res.status(401).json({ message: 'Authentication failed' });

}

jwt.verify(token, secretKey, (err, decoded) => {

if (err) {

return res.status(401).json({ message: 'Invalid token' });

}

// Attach user information to the request object

req.user = decoded;

next();

});

}
```

2. Input Validation and Sanitization

Ensure that all data received from clients or external sources is validated and sanitized to prevent injection attacks like SQL injection or cross-site scripting (XSS). Use libraries like express-validator to validate and sanitize user inputs.

```javascript
import { body, validationResult } from 'express-validator';

// Input validation middleware
```

```
const validateInputs = [

body('email').isEmail(),

body('password').isLength({ min: 8 }),

// Add more validation rules as needed

];

// Route handler

app.post('/register', validateInputs, (req, res) => {

const errors = validationResult(req);

if (!errors.isEmpty()) {

return res.status(400).json({ errors: errors.array() });

}

// Process registration logic

});
```

3. Data Encryption and Storage

Protect sensitive data at rest by encrypting it using industry-standard encryption algorithms. Use secure storage mechanisms and apply access controls to limit data exposure. Additionally, avoid storing sensitive data like passwords in plain text; instead, hash them securely.

```
import crypto from 'crypto';

// Data encryption

function encryptData(data: string, key: string): string {
```

```
const cipher = crypto.createCipher('aes-256-cbc', key);

let encrypted = cipher.update(data, 'utf8', 'hex');

encrypted += cipher.final('hex');

return encrypted;

}
```

4. Logging and Monitoring

Implement comprehensive logging to record important events and potential security incidents. Regularly review logs for unusual activities. Additionally, set up monitoring and alerting to detect and respond to security breaches in real-time.

```
// Winston logger for logging

import winston from 'winston';

const logger = winston.createLogger({

level: 'info',

format: winston.format.json(),

transports: [

new winston.transports.File({ filename: 'error.log', level: 'error' }),

new winston.transports.File({ filename: 'combined.log' }),

],

});

// Log an error
```

logger.error('This is an error message.');

5. Secure Dependencies

Keep all dependencies and libraries up to date to patch known vulnerabilities. Use tools like npm audit or yarn audit to identify vulnerable dependencies and apply updates promptly.

 # Check for vulnerabilities in npm packages

npm audit

6. Regular Security Audits

Perform security audits and penetration testing regularly to identify and address vulnerabilities in your TypeScript backend. Employ tools like OWASP ZAP or Nessus for automated security scans and manual testing.

 # Running OWASP ZAP security scan

zap-cli —start-url http://your-backend-url -d -quick-scan

By following these best practices, TypeScript developers can create robust and secure backends that protect data and ensure the integrity of their applications. Security is an ongoing process, and staying informed about the latest threats and security practices is essential to maintaining a secure backend environment.

Section 17.4: Penetration Testing and Vulnerability Assessment

Penetration testing, often referred to as ethical hacking, is a proactive approach to identifying and addressing vulnerabilities in your TypeScript applications and backend systems. In this section, we'll delve into the importance of penetration testing and how to perform vulnerability assessments effectively.

1. The Importance of Penetration Testing

Penetration testing is a critical component of a robust security strategy. Its primary objectives include:

- Identifying vulnerabilities: Penetration testers simulate real-world attacks to uncover security weaknesses that may go unnoticed otherwise.

- Measuring the impact: Testers assess the potential damage and exploitability of vulnerabilities.

- Providing recommendations: After testing, a report is generated with recommendations on how to mitigate identified vulnerabilities.

2. Types of Penetration Testing

There are various types of penetration testing, each serving specific purposes:

- **Black Box Testing**: Testers have no prior knowledge of the application or system. They simulate external attackers.

- **White Box Testing**: Testers have complete knowledge of the application or system, often including source code. This type focuses on verifying code-level vulnerabilities.

- **Gray Box Testing**: Testers have limited knowledge of the application or system. This approach strikes a balance between black box and white box testing.

3. Conducting Penetration Testing

Here's an overview of the steps involved in conducting penetration testing:

a. Planning and Scoping

Define the scope of the test, including target systems, testing methods, and objectives. Identify any legal or compliance requirements.

b. Information Gathering

Gather information about the target, such as network architecture, application details, and potential vulnerabilities.

c. Vulnerability Analysis

Identify known vulnerabilities and weaknesses that may be exploited.

d. Exploitation

Attempt to exploit identified vulnerabilities, mimicking real-world attackers. This step requires a deep understanding of attack techniques.

e. Post-Exploitation

Assess the consequences of successful exploitation and determine the extent of potential damage.

f. Reporting

Compile the results and provide a detailed report that includes identified vulnerabilities, potential impact, and recommended remediation steps.

4. Vulnerability Assessment Tools

Several tools can assist in penetration testing and vulnerability assessment:

- **Nessus**: A comprehensive vulnerability scanner that identifies security vulnerabilities in networks and web applications.

- **OWASP ZAP**: An open-source security testing tool for finding vulnerabilities in web applications during development and testing.

- **Metasploit**: A widely used penetration testing framework that aids in identifying, verifying, and exploiting vulnerabilities.

5. Regulatory Compliance

Penetration testing is often required to meet regulatory compliance standards, such as the Payment Card Industry Data Security Standard (PCI DSS) or the Health Insurance Portability and Accountability Act (HIPAA). Compliance regulations typically mandate regular testing to ensure the security of sensitive data.

6. Continuous Testing

Security is an ongoing process. Regular penetration testing helps organizations stay ahead of emerging threats and vulnerabilities.

Consider incorporating penetration testing into your software development lifecycle to identify and address security issues early.

In conclusion, penetration testing and vulnerability assessment are vital components of a robust security strategy. By simulating real-world attacks and identifying vulnerabilities, organizations can proactively secure their TypeScript applications and backend systems, reducing the risk of data breaches and other security incidents.

Section 17.5: Security Libraries and Tools for TypeScript

Ensuring the security of your TypeScript applications is paramount in today's interconnected world. In this section, we'll explore various security libraries and tools available for TypeScript developers to bolster the security of their applications.

1. Libraries for Input Validation

Input validation is a fundamental aspect of security. Properly validated input helps prevent common vulnerabilities like SQL injection and cross-site scripting (XSS). Here are some TypeScript libraries to assist with input validation:

- **validator.js**[1]: A library for string validation, including sanitization, escaping, and more.

import { isEmail } **from** 'validator';

const isValidEmail = isEmail('example@email.com'); // *Returns true if it's a valid email.*

---

1. **https://github.com/validatorjs/validator.js**

- **joi**[2]: A schema description language and data validator for JavaScript and TypeScript.

```
import Joi from 'joi';

const schema = Joi.object({

username: Joi.string().alphanum().min(3).max(30).required(),

password: Joi.string().pattern(new RegExp('^[a-zA-Z0-9]{3,30}$')),

});

const { error, value } = schema.validate({ username: 'example', password: '123456' });
```

2. Authentication and Authorization Libraries

Securing user authentication and authorization is a crucial part of application security. TypeScript offers libraries that simplify these tasks:

- **Passport**[3]: A widely used authentication middleware for Node.js applications.

```
import passport from 'passport';

// Define a strategy

passport.use(new LocalStrategy(

(username, password, done) => {

// Authentication logic here
```

---

2. https://github.com/sideway/joi

3. http://www.passportjs.org/

```
}

));
```

// Authenticate a request

```
app.post('/login', passport.authenticate('local', {

successRedirect: '/',

failureRedirect: '/login',

}));
```

- **jsonwebtoken**[4]: A library for working with JSON Web Tokens (JWTs), commonly used for authorization.

```
import jwt from 'jsonwebtoken';

const token = jwt.sign({ userId: 123 }, 'secretKey', { expiresIn: '1h' });

const decoded = jwt.verify(token, 'secretKey');
```

3. Security Scanners

Regularly scanning your code and dependencies for security vulnerabilities is crucial. Here are some tools that can help:

- **npm audit**[5]: Built into npm, it checks your project for vulnerabilities in its dependencies.

```
npm audit
```

- **Snyk**[6]: A tool that scans your project for vulnerabilities and offers remediation advice.

---

4. https://github.com/auth0/node-jsonwebtoken

5. https://docs.npmjs.com/cli/v7/commands/npm-audit

npx snyk test

4. Content Security Policy (CSP)

Implementing CSP headers in your web application can mitigate the risk of XSS attacks. TypeScript developers can define CSP policies in their web applications to control which resources can be loaded.

<**meta http-equiv**="Content-Security-Policy" **content**="default-src 'self'; script-src 'self' 'unsafe-inline'">

5. Web Application Firewalls (WAFs)

Consider using a WAF to protect your web application from common security threats, such as SQL injection and XSS attacks. Popular cloud providers like AWS, Azure, and Google Cloud offer WAF services that can be integrated with your TypeScript applications.

6. Regular Security Training

Lastly, invest in regular security training for your development team. Knowledgeable developers are your first line of defense against security threats. Encourage them to stay updated on security best practices and emerging threats.

In conclusion, securing TypeScript applications is a multifaceted endeavor. By leveraging the right security libraries and tools, implementing best practices like input validation, authentication, and authorization, and staying informed about security threats, TypeScript developers can create robust and secure applications that protect user data and maintain user trust.

---

6. https://snyk.io/

Chapter 18: Internationalization and Localization

In an increasingly globalized world, catering to users from diverse linguistic and cultural backgrounds is essential. Internationalization (i18n) and localization (l10n) are the processes of adapting your TypeScript applications to support different languages and regions. In this chapter, we'll delve into the principles and techniques of internationalization and localization in TypeScript.

Section 18.1: Implementing Internationalization in TypeScript

Internationalization involves designing your application to be language-agnostic, allowing it to support multiple languages without code changes. TypeScript provides various tools and libraries to facilitate this process.

1. Internationalization Libraries

a. Format.js (react-intl)

Format.js[1] is a popular internationalization library for React applications, but it can be used with TypeScript in various scenarios. It offers features like date formatting, number formatting, and message translations.

To get started with Format.js in a TypeScript project, you can install the necessary packages:

npm install react-intl

---

1. https://formatjs.io/docs/getting-started/introduction

Here's a simple example of using Format.js for message translation:

```tsx
import React from 'react';

import { useIntl, FormattedMessage } from 'react-intl';

const MyComponent: React.FC = () => {

const intl = useIntl();

return (

<div>

<h1>

<FormattedMessage id="app.title" defaultMessage="My App" />

</h1>

<p>

<FormattedMessage

id="app.greeting"

defaultMessage="Hello, {name}!"

values={{ name: 'Alice' }}

/>

</p>

</div>

);

};
```

```
export default MyComponent;
```

b. *i18next*

i18next[2] is a comprehensive internationalization framework that can be used in TypeScript projects, including both web and backend applications. It supports key-value translation, interpolation, and more.

To get started with i18next, you can install the necessary packages:

```
npm install i18next i18next-browser-languagedetector i18next-xhr-backend
```

Here's a basic example of using i18next for translation in a TypeScript application:

```
import i18n from 'i18next';

import { initReactI18next } from 'react-i18next';

i18n

.use(initReactI18next)

.init({

lng: 'en', // Default language

resources: {

en: {

translation: {

greeting: 'Hello, {{name}}!',
```

---

2. https://www.i18next.com/

```
// ...

},

},

fr: {

translation: {

greeting: 'Bonjour, {{name}} !',

// ...

},

},

},

});
```

export default i18n;

Then, in your React components, you can use the useTranslation hook or the withTranslation higher-order component to access translations.

2. Message Extraction and Management

In TypeScript, it's common to extract messages to be translated from the source code. Tools like babel-plugin-react-intl[3] and react-scripts[4] provide extraction capabilities. You can also use ts-translate[5] for managing translations in a structured way.

---

3. https://github.com/formatjs/formatjs/tree/main/packages/babel-plugin-react-intl

4. https://github.com/facebook/create-react-app/tree/main/packages/react-scripts

5. https://github.com/primefaces/ts-translate

 # Extract messages with babel-plugin-react-intl

npm install babel-plugin-react-intl

 # Extract messages with react-scripts (Create React App)

npm install react-scripts

These tools enable you to mark messages in your code for translation and generate JSON files containing translations for different languages.

3. Choosing the Right Approach

When implementing internationalization in TypeScript, consider the specific needs of your project. Factors like the framework you're using, the size of your application, and your team's familiarity with different libraries can influence your choice of internationalization tools and techniques.

In conclusion, internationalization and localization are essential aspects of modern software development, especially for applications with a global user base. TypeScript, with its strong typing and support for modern JavaScript frameworks, is well-suited for building internationalized applications. By selecting the right internationalization libraries and following best practices, you can create software that welcomes users from diverse linguistic backgrounds and regions.

Section 18.2: Handling Multiple Languages and Cultures

When implementing internationalization and localization (i18n and l10n) in TypeScript applications, handling multiple languages and cultures effectively is a crucial aspect. In this section, we'll explore strategies and best practices for managing different languages and cultural preferences within your TypeScript codebase.

1. Language and Locale Identification

Before diving into handling multiple languages, it's essential to understand how to identify a user's language and locale preferences. The user's language preference is usually determined by their browser settings or a language selection feature in your application. Additionally, the locale represents the user's cultural and regional preferences, including date and time formats, currency symbols, and more.

In TypeScript, you can access the user's language and locale preferences through the navigator object in a web application. Here's an example of how to obtain the user's language and locale:

const userLanguage = navigator.language; // *e.g., "en-US"*

const userLocale = navigator.languages[0]; // *e.g., "en-US"*

Once you've determined the user's language and locale, you can use this information to load the appropriate translations and formats.

2. Language Files and Bundling

To handle multiple languages effectively, it's common to create separate language files or modules containing translations for each supported language. These language files can be JSON, JavaScript modules, or any other suitable format. Here's a basic example of how a language file might look:

// **en.json (English)**

{

```
"greeting": "Hello, {{name}}!",

// ...

}
```

```
// fr.json (French)

{

"greeting": "Bonjour, {{name}} !",

// ...

}
```

In your TypeScript application, you can load the appropriate language file based on the user's preferences. Tools like i18next and Format.js provide mechanisms for dynamically loading language resources at runtime.

3. Dynamic Language Switching

Allowing users to switch between languages dynamically is a user-friendly feature. You can implement a language switcher in your TypeScript application that updates the user's language preference and reloads the appropriate translations and formats. Ensure that the switcher is easily accessible, such as in a settings menu or header.

Here's a simplified example of a language switcher in a React component using i18next:

```
import React from 'react';

import { useTranslation } from 'react-i18next';

const LanguageSwitcher: React.FC = () => {
```

```
const { i18n } = useTranslation();

const changeLanguage = (newLanguage: string) => {

i18n.changeLanguage(newLanguage);

};

return (

<div>

<button                        onClick={()                        =>
changeLanguage('en')}>English</button>

<button                        onClick={()                        =>
changeLanguage('fr')}>Français</button>

{/* Add more language buttons as needed */}

</div>

);

};

export default LanguageSwitcher;
```

4. Consideration for Right-to-Left (RTL) Languages

When supporting languages that are written from right to left (e.g., Arabic or Hebrew), consider the layout adjustments required for these languages. Your TypeScript application should adapt its layout, alignment, and text direction to provide a seamless experience for RTL language users.

In conclusion, handling multiple languages and cultures in TypeScript applications involves identifying user preferences, organizing language files, enabling dynamic language switching, and considering RTL language support. By implementing these best practices, you can create inclusive applications that cater to a diverse international audience.

Section 18.3: Date, Time, and Currency Handling

When developing internationalized TypeScript applications, handling date, time, and currency formats in a way that aligns with users' cultural preferences is essential. In this section, we'll explore techniques and best practices for managing these aspects effectively.

1. Date and Time Formatting

Different regions have various date and time formats, including date order (e.g., MM/DD/YYYY or DD/MM/YYYY), time notation (e.g., 12-hour or 24-hour clock), and date separators. TypeScript provides the Intl.DateTimeFormat object, which is highly suitable for formatting dates and times according to user preferences.

Here's an example of formatting a date using Intl.DateTimeFormat:

```typescript
const date = new Date('2023-11-25T14:30:00');

const userLocale = 'en-US'; // User's locale

const formattedDate = new Intl.DateTimeFormat(userLocale).format(date);

console.log(formattedDate); // Output varies based on the user's locale
```

By specifying the user's locale, you can ensure that the date and time are presented correctly.

2. Currency Formatting

When displaying currency values, it's crucial to format them appropriately for the user's region. TypeScript provides the Intl.NumberFormat object, which allows you to format currency values according to the user's locale.

Here's an example of formatting currency:

const currencyValue = 12345.67;

const userLocale = 'en-US'; // *User's locale*

const currencyFormatter = **new** Intl.NumberFormat(userLocale, {

style: 'currency',

currency: 'USD', // *Currency code (e.g., USD for US Dollar)*

});

const formattedCurrency = currencyFormatter.format(currencyValue);

console.log(formattedCurrency); // *Output varies based on the user's locale*

By specifying the currency code and user locale, you can format currency values correctly.

3. Handling Time Zones

When dealing with date and time information, be aware of time zones. Ensure that you properly handle time zone conversions and provide users with options to select their time zone if necessary. The Intl.DateTimeFormat object can also be configured to include time zone information.

```typescript
const date = new Date('2023-11-25T14:30:00');

const userLocale = 'en-US'; // User's locale

const timeZone = 'America/New_York'; // User's time zone

const options = {

timeZoneName: 'short', // Display short time zone name (e.g., EST)

};

const formattedDate = new Intl.DateTimeFormat(userLocale, options).format(date);

console.log(formattedDate); // Output includes time zone information
```

4. Libraries for Date and Time Handling

For more advanced date and time operations, consider using libraries like date-fns, luxon, or moment-timezone. These libraries provide additional features and make it easier to work with dates, times, and time zones in TypeScript applications.

In conclusion, handling date, time, and currency formats in internationalized TypeScript applications requires using the Intl.DateTimeFormat and Intl.NumberFormat objects, considering time zones, and selecting appropriate libraries for complex date and time operations. By following these best practices, you can ensure that your application meets the cultural expectations of users from different regions.

Section 18.4: Accessibility Considerations

Accessibility is a critical aspect of TypeScript applications, ensuring that they can be used by people with disabilities. When developing internationalized applications, it's essential to consider accessibility to provide an inclusive user experience. In this section, we'll explore key accessibility considerations in TypeScript development.

1. Semantic HTML

Using semantic HTML elements is fundamental for accessibility. Ensure that you use appropriate HTML tags to convey the structure and meaning of your content. For example, use headings (<h1>, <h2>, etc.) to outline the document's structure and provide meaningful alt text for images.

<!—Semantic HTML example—>

<h1>Welcome to our internationalized website**</h1>**

<img src="flag.png" **alt**="Flag of the United States">

<p>This is the homepage of our website.**</p>**

2. ARIA Attributes

The Accessible Rich Internet Applications (ARIA) specification provides attributes that can be added to HTML elements to enhance accessibility for screen readers and assistive technologies. TypeScript developers should be familiar with ARIA attributes and use them appropriately.

<!—Using ARIA attributes for a button—>

<button aria-label="Close" **onclick**="closeDialog()">X**</button>**

3. Keyboard Navigation

Ensure that all interactive elements can be accessed and operated using a keyboard. Test your application's keyboard navigation to verify that users can navigate through menus, forms, and other components without relying on a mouse.

4. Focus Management

Proper focus management is crucial. When opening modal dialogs or dropdown menus, ensure that focus is trapped within the modal until it is closed. This prevents users from accidentally tabbing out of the modal.

```typescript
// TypeScript code for managing focus within a modal

const modal = document.getElementById('myModal');

modal.addEventListener('keydown', (e) => {

if (e.key === 'Tab' && !e.shiftKey) {

// Handle forward tab key press

e.preventDefault();

// Move focus to the next focusable element within the modal

}

});
```

5. Language Attributes

Include the lang attribute in your HTML to specify the language of the content. This helps screen readers and other assistive technologies understand the text's language.

```
<html lang="en-US">

<!—...—>

</html>
```

6. Testing with Assistive Technologies

Regularly test your TypeScript application with screen readers and other assistive technologies to ensure that it provides a meaningful and usable experience for users with disabilities.

7. Documentation and Training

Educate your development team about accessibility best practices and guidelines. Provide documentation on how to create accessible components and conduct accessibility audits as part of your development process.

8. User Testing

Involve users with disabilities in the testing phase of your application. Their feedback can help identify and address accessibility issues that may not be apparent during development.

In conclusion, accessibility should be an integral part of TypeScript development, especially when building internationalized applications. By following these accessibility considerations, you can create applications that are usable and inclusive for a diverse range of users, regardless of their abilities or cultural backgrounds.

Section 18.5: Case Studies: Global Apps with TypeScript

In this section, we'll explore real-world case studies of applications that have successfully leveraged TypeScript to create global apps. These case studies highlight how TypeScript's features and best practices can be applied to build internationalized and localized applications that cater to diverse audiences.

1. E-Commerce Platform Expansion

One case study involves an e-commerce platform that expanded its services globally. They used TypeScript to handle multi-language support and localization. By defining translation files for different languages and regions, they were able to dynamically switch content and provide a seamless shopping experience for users worldwide. TypeScript's strong typing helped catch translation-related issues during development.

2. Healthcare Management System

A healthcare management system used TypeScript to develop a comprehensive solution for healthcare providers in various countries. TypeScript's type safety proved invaluable in ensuring that sensitive patient data was handled securely and in compliance with different data protection regulations worldwide.

3. Social Networking App

A social networking app aimed to connect users from different countries. TypeScript was employed to manage language preferences, time zones, and culturally sensitive content. Additionally, they used TypeScript for real-time chat features, ensuring efficient communication across borders.

4. Educational Platform

An educational platform used TypeScript to create a global learning environment. TypeScript's support for modularization and code splitting helped optimize the platform's performance for users in regions with limited internet connectivity. It also facilitated the easy addition of new courses and content for different languages.

5. Financial Services Application

A financial services application extended its reach to international markets. TypeScript played a vital role in managing currency conversion, compliance with financial regulations in various countries, and ensuring the application's security. TypeScript's robust error-checking helped identify potential financial risks during development.

6. Travel Booking Portal

A travel booking portal utilized TypeScript to provide a user-friendly experience for travelers worldwide. TypeScript's strong type checking helped prevent booking errors and ensure accurate pricing and availability information for different destinations. It also enabled seamless integration with third-party travel services.

7. Non-Profit Organization Website

A non-profit organization's website used TypeScript to engage donors and supporters from diverse backgrounds. TypeScript helped manage content in multiple languages and allowed the organization to share stories and impact reports effectively. The website also leveraged TypeScript for donation processing and secure data handling.

8. Video Streaming Platform

A video streaming platform expanded its audience by supporting content creators and viewers from various countries. TypeScript's performance optimization features ensured smooth streaming experiences, while its internationalization capabilities allowed for subtitles and content descriptions in multiple languages.

In these case studies, TypeScript demonstrated its versatility and effectiveness in building global applications. By following best practices and leveraging TypeScript's features for internationalization, localization, and error prevention, these applications successfully reached and engaged users worldwide. These examples illustrate how TypeScript can be a powerful tool for developers aiming to create global apps that cater to diverse cultures and regions.

Chapter 19: TypeScript and IoT Development

Section 19.1: TypeScript in the Internet of Things (IoT)

The Internet of Things (IoT) refers to the interconnected network of devices, sensors, and objects that communicate and exchange data over the internet. IoT has gained significant traction across various industries, including home automation, healthcare, manufacturing, and agriculture. TypeScript can be a valuable tool for developing IoT applications, offering benefits like type safety, scalability, and code maintainability. In this section, we'll explore how TypeScript can be used effectively in IoT development.

Understanding IoT Development

IoT development involves creating software that runs on embedded devices, sensors, and gateways. These devices collect data, process it locally, and often send it to the cloud for further analysis. TypeScript can be used to build both the firmware that runs on IoT devices and the cloud-based applications that manage and analyze the data.

Benefits of Using TypeScript in IoT

1. **Type Safety**: TypeScript's strong type system helps catch errors at compile-time, reducing the likelihood of runtime errors in critical IoT applications. This is particularly important in environments where reliability and safety are paramount.
2. **Scalability**: IoT ecosystems can grow rapidly, and TypeScript's modularization and organization features

make it easier to manage and scale your codebase as your IoT network expands.

3. **Code Maintainability**: TypeScript's code readability and maintainability features, such as interfaces and classes, make it easier to develop and maintain IoT software over time.

4. **Ecosystem Compatibility**: TypeScript can be used with popular IoT development platforms and frameworks, making it accessible to a wide range of IoT developers.

Use Cases for TypeScript in IoT

1. **Smart Home Automation**: TypeScript can be used to build firmware for smart home devices like thermostats, lights, and locks. Its type safety ensures that these devices operate reliably and securely.

2. **Industrial IoT (IIoT)**: In industrial settings, TypeScript can be used to develop software for monitoring and controlling machines, ensuring efficient and safe operations.

3. **Healthcare IoT**: TypeScript's safety features make it suitable for healthcare IoT devices that collect and transmit patient data. It can help ensure the accuracy and privacy of medical information.

4. **Agriculture IoT**: TypeScript can be used in agriculture IoT solutions to monitor soil conditions, automate irrigation, and collect data from sensors on farms.

Challenges in IoT Development with TypeScript

While TypeScript offers many advantages, IoT development also presents unique challenges:

1. **Resource Constraints**: IoT devices often have limited processing power and memory. TypeScript code must be optimized for resource efficiency.
2. **Connectivity Issues**: IoT devices may operate in environments with intermittent or unreliable internet connectivity. TypeScript applications must handle these conditions gracefully.
3. **Security**: IoT devices are susceptible to security threats. TypeScript developers must implement robust security measures to protect against unauthorized access and data breaches.

In summary, TypeScript is a valuable choice for IoT development, offering type safety, scalability, and code maintainability. It can be used across various IoT use cases, from smart home automation to industrial applications. However, developers must also address the unique challenges of resource constraints, connectivity issues, and security to create reliable and secure IoT solutions.

Section 19.2: Building IoT Applications with TypeScript

In the previous section, we discussed the benefits of using TypeScript in IoT development and explored various use cases where TypeScript can be applied effectively. Now, let's delve deeper into building IoT applications with TypeScript, covering key considerations, tools, and best practices.

Selecting IoT Hardware and Platforms

Building IoT applications starts with selecting the right hardware and platforms. When choosing IoT hardware, consider factors such as sensors, connectivity options (Wi-Fi, Bluetooth, LoRa, etc.), power requirements, and form factor. Additionally, you'll need to decide on the cloud platform for data storage, processing, and device management.

Setting Up the Development Environment

To develop IoT applications with TypeScript, you'll need a development environment that supports embedded systems. Some popular choices include:

- **PlatformIO**: An open-source ecosystem for IoT development that supports a wide range of development boards and platforms.

- **Arduino IDE**: If you're using Arduino-compatible devices, the Arduino IDE can be configured to work with TypeScript through custom build scripts.

- **Visual Studio Code**: VS Code is a versatile code editor that can be extended with IoT development extensions and TypeScript support.

Writing TypeScript Firmware

Writing firmware for IoT devices in TypeScript involves several steps:

1. **Configuring the Build System**: Set up the build system to compile TypeScript into JavaScript that can run on your target device. Depending on your platform, you may need to use tools like TSC (TypeScript Compiler) or custom build scripts.
2. **Accessing Hardware**: Use libraries and APIs provided by the IoT platform or hardware manufacturer to interact

with sensors, actuators, and communication modules.
TypeScript typings for these libraries can provide type
safety.

3. **Implementing IoT Protocols**: Depending on your IoT
    ecosystem, you may need to implement communication
    protocols such as MQTT, CoAP, or HTTP to send and
    receive data from IoT devices.

4. **Error Handling**: Implement error handling and recovery
    mechanisms to ensure the reliability of your IoT
    applications. TypeScript's type system can help catch errors
    at compile-time.

Managing IoT Devices

Managing IoT devices at scale is a critical aspect of IoT development.
Cloud platforms like AWS IoT, Google Cloud IoT, and Azure IoT
provide services for device management, data ingestion, and
analytics. TypeScript can be used to build device management
solutions that allow you to:

- Provision and configure devices remotely.

- Monitor device health and performance.

- Perform firmware updates and maintenance tasks.

Security Considerations

Security is a top priority in IoT development. TypeScript can help
enforce security best practices, such as:

- **Authentication and Authorization**: Implement secure
  authentication and authorization mechanisms to prevent
  unauthorized access to devices and data.

- **Data Encryption**: Use encryption to protect data both in transit and at rest. TypeScript libraries can provide cryptographic functions.

- **Secure Boot and Firmware Updates**: Ensure that devices have secure boot mechanisms and can receive signed firmware updates.

- **Regular Security Audits**: Periodically audit your IoT applications for vulnerabilities and apply security patches promptly.

Testing and Deployment

Before deploying IoT applications, thorough testing is essential. This includes unit testing of firmware components, integration testing of device interactions, and end-to-end testing of the entire IoT ecosystem. TypeScript testing frameworks like Jest can be used for this purpose.

Deployment of IoT applications involves physically installing devices, configuring cloud services, and monitoring the live system for performance and security issues.

In conclusion, TypeScript is a powerful choice for building IoT applications, offering type safety, code maintainability, and a robust development ecosystem. When developing IoT solutions with TypeScript, consider hardware selection, development environment setup, firmware development, device management, security measures, testing, and deployment strategies to create reliable and secure IoT systems.

Section 19.3: Interfacing with Hardware using TypeScript

Interfacing with hardware is at the core of IoT development. In this section, we will explore how TypeScript can be used to interface with hardware components such as sensors, actuators, and communication modules in IoT applications.

Choosing the Right Hardware Interface

IoT devices often rely on various hardware interfaces to interact with the physical world. The choice of interface depends on the specific requirements of your project. Some common hardware interfaces include:

- **GPIO (General-Purpose Input/Output)**: GPIO pins allow digital input and output, making them suitable for controlling LEDs, buttons, and simple sensors.

- **I2C (Inter-Integrated Circuit)**: I2C is a serial communication protocol used for connecting multiple sensors and devices to a single bus. TypeScript libraries can simplify I2C communication.

- **SPI (Serial Peripheral Interface)**: SPI is another serial protocol for high-speed communication with devices like displays and flash memory.

- **UART (Universal Asynchronous Receiver-Transmitter)**: UART is used for serial communication between devices, often for communication with external modules like GPS receivers.

TypeScript Libraries for Hardware Interfacing

To interface with hardware using TypeScript, you can leverage various libraries and frameworks tailored to different IoT platforms and hardware components. Some popular TypeScript libraries and tools include:

- **Johnny-Five**: Johnny-Five is a JavaScript and TypeScript framework for working with Arduino and other platforms. It provides an easy-to-use API for interacting with sensors and actuators.

- **rpio**: This TypeScript library is designed for Raspberry Pi GPIO access. It enables you to control GPIO pins for various applications.

- **node-i2c-bus**: If you're working with I2C devices, this library simplifies I2C communication in TypeScript. It supports multiple I2C buses and devices.

- **pigpio**: pigpio is a library for Raspberry Pi that provides low-level access to GPIO pins and PWM (Pulse Width Modulation) control. While it's primarily written in C, you can use TypeScript bindings to access its functionality.

Example: Interfacing with a Temperature Sensor

Let's walk through a simple example of interfacing with a temperature sensor using TypeScript and the Johnny-Five library. In this scenario, we'll assume you're working with an Arduino board and a digital temperature sensor (e.g., DHT11 or DHT22).

```typescript
import { Board, Thermometer } from 'johnny-five';
```

```
const board = new Board();

board.on('ready', () => {

const thermometer = new Thermometer({

controller: 'DHT11', // Use the appropriate controller for your sensor

pin: 2, // Specify the GPIO pin where the sensor is connected

});

thermometer.on('change', () => {

console.log(`Temperature: ${thermometer.celsius}°C`);

});

});
```

In this example, we import Johnny-Five, set up the board, and create
a Thermometer instance to interface with the temperature sensor.
When the sensor's value changes, we log the temperature in Celsius
to the console.

Advanced Hardware Interfacing

For more complex IoT projects, you may need to interface with
a combination of sensors, actuators, and communication modules.
TypeScript's strong typing and modular structure make it well-suited
for managing complex hardware interactions.

Remember that proper error handling, data processing, and
calibration are essential when working with hardware. Additionally,
consult the documentation and resources provided by your hardware
manufacturer to ensure correct usage and compatibility with
TypeScript.

In conclusion, TypeScript offers a reliable and structured approach to interfacing with hardware in IoT applications. By selecting the right hardware interfaces, using appropriate libraries, and following best practices, you can build robust and efficient IoT systems with TypeScript.

Section 19.4: Networking and Communication in IoT

Networking and communication are fundamental aspects of IoT development, enabling devices to exchange data, control commands, and interact with cloud services and other devices. In this section, we'll explore how TypeScript can be used for networking and communication in IoT applications.

IoT Communication Protocols

IoT devices use various communication protocols to interact with each other and external services. Some common IoT communication protocols include:

- **MQTT (Message Queuing Telemetry Transport)**: MQTT is a lightweight publish-subscribe messaging protocol commonly used in IoT. It's efficient for low-bandwidth, high-latency, or unreliable networks.

- **HTTP/HTTPS**: Many IoT devices communicate with cloud services or web applications using HTTP or its secure counterpart, HTTPS. RESTful APIs are often used for data exchange.

- **CoAP (Constrained Application Protocol)**: CoAP is designed for resource-constrained devices in IoT. It's suitable for simple, low-power devices.

- **WebSocket**: WebSocket provides full-duplex communication channels over a single TCP connection. It's useful for real-time applications and device-to-device communication.

TypeScript Libraries for IoT Communication

To implement IoT communication in TypeScript, you can leverage various libraries and tools that simplify network interactions. Some popular options include:

- **MQTT.js**: This library allows TypeScript applications to connect to MQTT brokers and publish/subscribe to topics. It's suitable for MQTT-based IoT projects.

- **axios**: Axios is a popular HTTP client for TypeScript and JavaScript. It simplifies making HTTP requests to RESTful APIs, making it handy for IoT devices that communicate with web services.

- **node-coap**: If you're working with CoAP, this TypeScript library provides an easy way to create CoAP clients and servers.

- **WebSocket libraries**: There are several WebSocket libraries available for TypeScript, such as 'ws' and 'socket.io-client,' which facilitate WebSocket communication.

Example: MQTT Communication

Let's illustrate IoT communication with TypeScript by creating a simple MQTT publisher and subscriber using the 'mqtt' library:

```typescript
import * as mqtt from 'mqtt';

// MQTT broker URL

const brokerUrl = 'mqtt://mqtt.eclipse.org';

// Create a client

const client = mqtt.connect(brokerUrl);

// Connect to the broker

client.on('connect', () => {

console.log('Connected to MQTT broker');

// Publish a message

client.publish('iot/topic', 'Hello, MQTT!');

});

// Subscribe to a topic

client.subscribe('iot/topic');

// Handle incoming messages

client.on('message', (topic, message) => {

console.log(`Received message on topic ${topic}: ${message.toString()}`);

});
```

In this example, we import the 'mqtt' library and create an MQTT client. We connect to an MQTT broker, publish a message, and subscribe to a topic. When a message arrives on the subscribed topic, we print it to the console.

Secure Communication

Security is crucial in IoT, especially when transmitting sensitive data. Ensure that your IoT communication is secured using appropriate encryption, authentication, and authorization mechanisms. Consider using HTTPS, TLS/SSL for MQTT, and other secure protocols to protect your IoT devices and data.

In conclusion, TypeScript provides a versatile platform for implementing networking and communication in IoT applications. By choosing the right communication protocols, using TypeScript libraries, and following security best practices, you can build robust and efficient IoT systems that seamlessly exchange data with other devices and services.

Section 19.5: Real-world TypeScript IoT Project Examples

In this section, we'll delve into real-world examples of TypeScript-based IoT projects to showcase how TypeScript can be applied to create practical IoT solutions. These examples illustrate the versatility and capabilities of TypeScript in IoT development.

1. Smart Home Automation System

Description: A smart home automation system built with TypeScript controls various home devices such as lights, thermostats, and security cameras. TypeScript is used for developing the backend server and the frontend user interface.

Implementation: TypeScript facilitates the creation of a Node.js backend that communicates with IoT devices using MQTT or HTTP. The frontend, built with TypeScript and a framework like Angular or React, allows homeowners to control and monitor devices remotely through a web or mobile app.

2. Environmental Monitoring Station

Description: An environmental monitoring station built with TypeScript collects data on air quality, temperature, humidity, and more. The data is sent to a cloud service for analysis and visualization.

Implementation: TypeScript is used to program the IoT sensors and microcontrollers, such as Raspberry Pi or Arduino, responsible for data collection. Data is transmitted securely to the cloud via MQTT or HTTPS. TypeScript can be used to develop serverless functions for real-time data processing and storage in cloud platforms like AWS Lambda or Azure Functions.

3. Fleet Management System

Description: A fleet management system for tracking and optimizing vehicles in a logistics company. TypeScript is utilized for both the embedded GPS tracking devices and the web-based management platform.

Implementation: TypeScript is employed to program the GPS tracking devices' microcontrollers, ensuring accurate location data transmission over cellular or satellite networks. On the server side, TypeScript handles real-time data ingestion and storage in databases like MongoDB or PostgreSQL. The web-based management platform, built with TypeScript and a framework like Vue.js, provides real-time tracking and reporting.

4. Agriculture Automation

Description: TypeScript is used in an agriculture automation project that involves controlling irrigation systems, monitoring soil conditions, and managing crop growth.

Implementation: TypeScript enables the development of IoT controllers for irrigation pumps, soil sensors, and actuators that control valves and pumps. These controllers communicate via MQTT or CoAP to optimize irrigation based on real-time soil data. TypeScript is also used for a dashboard that visualizes soil conditions and irrigation status.

5. Industrial IoT (IIoT) for Predictive Maintenance

Description: An IIoT solution for predictive maintenance in industrial machinery. TypeScript is used to collect data from sensors, analyze it, and predict equipment failures.

Implementation: TypeScript is employed in IoT devices attached to industrial machinery. These devices collect data on temperature, vibration, and other indicators. TypeScript is used for data preprocessing, analytics, and machine learning models for predictive maintenance. When anomalies are detected, alerts are sent through MQTT or WebSocket for immediate action.

6. Wildlife Conservation and Tracking

Description: TypeScript is used in a wildlife conservation project to track and monitor animal movements. IoT devices are attached to animals for location tracking.

Implementation: TypeScript is utilized to program the GPS and communication modules in animal tracking collars. These devices transmit location data periodically to a central server, which uses

TypeScript for data processing, geofencing, and generating reports on animal movements. Researchers access this data through a TypeScript-powered web application.

These real-world examples demonstrate how TypeScript can be applied across various IoT domains, from home automation and environmental monitoring to logistics and wildlife conservation. TypeScript's versatility, strong typing system, and ability to work with both frontend and backend technologies make it a valuable choice for IoT development, enabling developers to build robust and efficient IoT solutions.

Chapter 20: The Future of TypeScript

Section 20.1: TypeScript's Place in the Future of Development

TypeScript has established itself as a prominent and influential player in the world of web development. As we look ahead, it's essential to consider TypeScript's role in shaping the future of software development. In this section, we'll explore the significance of TypeScript in the evolving landscape of programming languages and development practices.

1. Growth and Popularity

TypeScript's growth trajectory is remarkable. It has consistently gained popularity among developers, reflecting the community's trust and the language's utility. As TypeScript continues to evolve, its community of contributors and users expands, reinforcing its position as a leading language for web development.

2. Integration with Emerging Technologies

TypeScript is well-suited to adapt to emerging technologies. Its strong typing system, tooling support, and ability to compile to JavaScript ensure that TypeScript remains relevant in the context of modern web development. As new technologies and paradigms emerge, TypeScript is likely to play a vital role in their adoption and integration.

3. TypeScript in the Backend

While TypeScript's primary use case has been frontend web development, its influence in backend development is growing.

Frameworks like Nest.js have gained popularity, providing a TypeScript-first approach to building server-side applications. This trend suggests that TypeScript's presence in full-stack development will continue to expand.

4. Collaboration and Interoperability

TypeScript's commitment to interoperability with JavaScript is a strategic advantage. It allows developers to gradually adopt TypeScript into existing projects, easing migration efforts. Furthermore, TypeScript fosters collaboration between frontend and backend teams by enabling them to share types and interfaces, resulting in more robust and efficient codebases.

5. Enhanced Tooling

TypeScript's ecosystem benefits from a rich set of tools and integrations. IDEs like Visual Studio Code offer exceptional TypeScript support, making it an attractive choice for developers. As tooling continues to improve, the development experience with TypeScript is expected to become even more efficient.

6. Community-Driven Innovation

The open-source nature of TypeScript ensures continuous innovation. Community-driven proposals and contributions shape the language's evolution. This collaborative approach enhances TypeScript's adaptability to industry trends and best practices.

7. TypeScript Beyond the Web

TypeScript's applicability extends beyond web development. It is increasingly used in other domains, including mobile app development, IoT, and game development. TypeScript's versatility positions it as a versatile language for diverse software projects.

In conclusion, TypeScript's future appears bright and promising. Its growth, adaptability, and strong community support position it as a key player in the ever-evolving field of software development. As the technology landscape continues to evolve, TypeScript is poised to remain a driving force in shaping the way we build web and software applications. Developers can anticipate exciting opportunities and challenges as TypeScript continues to influence the future of development practices.

Section 20.2: Emerging Trends and Technologies

In the ever-evolving landscape of web development, staying informed about emerging trends and technologies is crucial. As TypeScript developers, understanding these trends can help you make informed decisions about the tools, libraries, and practices you adopt. Let's explore some of the prominent emerging trends and technologies in the context of TypeScript.

1. Serverless Architecture

Serverless computing has gained traction as a cost-effective and scalable approach to building applications. With TypeScript's ability to compile to JavaScript compatible with serverless platforms like AWS Lambda and Azure Functions, it becomes a valuable language for serverless development. Its strong typing and tooling support can enhance the reliability of serverless functions.

2. WebAssembly (Wasm)

WebAssembly is revolutionizing web development by enabling high-performance code execution in web browsers. TypeScript can be transpiled to WebAssembly, opening up new possibilities for web applications that require intensive computations, such as gaming and multimedia processing. Developers can harness the power of TypeScript while taking advantage of Wasm's speed and efficiency.

3. Progressive Web Apps (PWAs)

Progressive Web Apps continue to gain momentum as they offer a seamless and responsive user experience across various devices. TypeScript's strong typing and modularization features align well with the development of PWAs. It allows developers to create maintainable and robust PWAs that can run offline and provide native-like experiences.

4. Micro-frontends

Micro-frontends have emerged as an architectural pattern for building complex web applications. TypeScript's support for code splitting and module systems makes it an excellent choice for implementing micro-frontends. Developers can create independent, reusable components using TypeScript, facilitating the development and maintenance of micro-frontend architectures.

5. Machine Learning and AI

Machine learning and artificial intelligence are permeating various domains, including web development. TypeScript can be used in conjunction with libraries like TensorFlow.js and Brain.js to build machine learning-powered web applications. Its static typing can catch errors at compile time, ensuring the correctness of machine learning code.

6. JAMstack Architecture

The JAMstack architecture, emphasizing decoupling front-end and back-end concerns, has gained popularity. TypeScript's ability to work seamlessly with various APIs and services aligns with the JAMstack approach. Developers can leverage TypeScript to build robust front-end applications that communicate with APIs, databases, and services.

7. Web3 and Blockchain Development

With the rise of blockchain technology and decentralized applications (dApps), TypeScript has found relevance in web3 development. Projects like Ethereum and Polkadot provide TypeScript libraries for building blockchain applications. TypeScript's safety features are advantageous in the context of smart contract development.

8. Cross-platform Development

TypeScript's cross-platform capabilities extend beyond web development. It can be used for cross-platform mobile app development using frameworks like React Native and Flutter. This allows developers to write a single codebase in TypeScript and target multiple platforms, reducing development time and effort.

9. Cloud-native Development

As cloud-native development practices continue to evolve, TypeScript remains relevant. Its compatibility with cloud platforms like AWS, Azure, and Google Cloud facilitates the development of cloud-native applications. TypeScript can be used to build serverless functions, APIs, and microservices in cloud environments.

In summary, TypeScript's adaptability and strong typing make it well-suited to embrace emerging trends and technologies in web and software development. Developers who invest in learning and leveraging TypeScript will find themselves well-equipped to tackle the challenges and opportunities presented by these evolving trends. Staying current with these technologies can help TypeScript developers remain at the forefront of the industry and continue to build innovative and impactful solutions.

Section 20.3: The Evolving TypeScript Ecosystem

The TypeScript ecosystem is continually evolving to meet the demands of modern web and software development. In this section, we'll explore the key aspects of this evolution, including tools, libraries, and community contributions.

1. TypeScript Releases and Updates

The TypeScript team at Microsoft maintains an active release cycle, consistently delivering updates and new features. Developers can stay up-to-date with the latest improvements by regularly checking for new TypeScript versions. Additionally, TypeScript follows the Semantic Versioning (SemVer) scheme, making it easier to understand the impact of updates on existing projects.

To check for updates and install the latest TypeScript version, you can use the following command with npm:

```
npm install -g typescript@latest
```

2. Editor Support

TypeScript enjoys robust support from popular code editors and IDEs, including Visual Studio Code, WebStorm, and Sublime Text. These editors offer features like autocompletion, type checking, and code navigation tailored for TypeScript. Visual Studio Code, in particular, provides excellent TypeScript integration and is widely favored by developers in the TypeScript community.

3. TypeScript Declaration Files

Declaration files (with a .d.ts extension) play a crucial role in the TypeScript ecosystem. They provide type information for JavaScript libraries and enable TypeScript to understand the shape of external code. The DefinitelyTyped repository hosts a vast collection of declaration files for popular libraries, making it easier to work with third-party code in TypeScript projects.

You can install declaration files for a specific library using npm, for example:

npm install—save @types/lodash

4. Build Tools and Bundlers

TypeScript can be seamlessly integrated into various build tools and bundlers, such as Webpack, Rollup, and Parcel. These tools enable efficient code splitting, tree shaking, and bundling of TypeScript code for production deployment. Webpack, in particular, has extensive TypeScript support, allowing you to configure TypeScript loaders and plugins.

5. Testing Frameworks

Testing is a fundamental aspect of software development, and TypeScript supports a range of testing frameworks like Jest, Mocha, and Jasmine. These frameworks offer TypeScript typings, making it easy to write type-safe tests for your codebase. You can also use libraries like ts-jest for enhanced TypeScript compatibility with Jest.

6. Code Quality Tools

Maintaining code quality is essential for large-scale TypeScript projects. Tools like TSLint and ESLint with TypeScript support can help enforce coding standards and catch potential issues early in the development process. The TypeScript team has also integrated some linting features directly into the TypeScript compiler, offering a unified solution for code quality checks.

7. Package Managers

TypeScript projects often rely on package managers like npm and Yarn to manage dependencies and facilitate collaboration. These package managers work seamlessly with TypeScript and enable you to install, update, and manage TypeScript packages efficiently.

8. Community Contributions

The TypeScript community is active and vibrant, with developers contributing to open-source projects, sharing knowledge, and providing valuable feedback. GitHub hosts the TypeScript repository, where you can report issues, suggest improvements, and track the language's development.

9. Third-party Libraries

The availability of TypeScript-compatible libraries and frameworks continues to grow. Many popular JavaScript libraries and frameworks, including React, Angular, and Vue, offer official TypeScript support. This ensures a smooth development experience when using TypeScript with these technologies.

10. Learning Resources

Numerous online resources, courses, and tutorials are available for developers looking to learn TypeScript. The TypeScript Handbook, maintained by the TypeScript team, is an excellent starting point for mastering the language. Additionally, community-driven websites and forums provide a platform for developers to seek help and share their expertise.

In conclusion, the TypeScript ecosystem is dynamic and continually adapting to the evolving needs of developers. Staying engaged with the TypeScript community, keeping your development tools up-to-date, and exploring new libraries and frameworks are essential for harnessing the full potential of TypeScript in modern software development. As the language and ecosystem evolve, TypeScript remains a powerful tool for building robust, maintainable, and scalable applications.

Section 20.4: Preparing for Future TypeScript Updates

As TypeScript evolves, it's important for developers to stay prepared for future updates and changes. The TypeScript team regularly introduces new features, improvements, and breaking changes to the language. Here are some strategies for effectively managing and adapting to future TypeScript updates:

1. Keep Your Dependencies Up-to-Date

One of the most crucial aspects of preparing for TypeScript updates is keeping your project's dependencies current. This includes not only TypeScript itself but also any libraries, tools, and packages your project relies on. Many updates are designed to work with the latest versions of related software, so staying up-to-date can help prevent compatibility issues.

To update TypeScript to the latest version, you can use npm or yarn as follows:

 # Using npm

npm install -g typescript@latest

 # Using yarn

yarn global add typescript@latest

For libraries and packages, regularly check for updates and apply them as needed. Many package managers provide commands to check for outdated dependencies and update them.

2. Monitor TypeScript Release Notes

The TypeScript team publishes detailed release notes for each new version. These notes contain information about new features, bug fixes, and breaking changes. Reviewing these release notes before updating can help you understand the impact of the update on your project.

You can find TypeScript release notes on the official GitHub repository in the "releases" section. Additionally, the TypeScript blog often provides in-depth explanations of major updates.

3. Use TSLint and TSLint-to-ESLint Migration

As of TypeScript 4.0, TSLint has been deprecated in favor of ESLint with TypeScript support. To prepare for this change, consider migrating your projects from TSLint to ESLint. ESLint offers TypeScript-specific rules and has a more active community, making it a solid choice for code linting.

To migrate from TSLint to ESLint, you can use the tslint-to-eslint-config tool, which automates much of the conversion process. Be sure to review and adjust your ESLint configuration to match your project's specific requirements.

4. Test Your Code

Before updating TypeScript, it's essential to thoroughly test your codebase to identify any potential issues. Automated tests, including unit tests, integration tests, and end-to-end tests, can help ensure that your application behaves as expected with the new TypeScript version.

Consider creating a dedicated branch or environment for testing TypeScript updates to avoid disrupting your main development workflow. This allows you to isolate any problems and address them without affecting ongoing development.

5. Maintain a Clear Upgrade Plan

Having a well-defined upgrade plan in place can streamline the process of transitioning to a new TypeScript version. Your plan should include steps for updating TypeScript and related tools, testing your application, and addressing any breaking changes.

Ensure that your team is aware of the upgrade plan and understands their roles in the process. Communication and collaboration among team members are essential to a successful update.

6. Community Involvement

The TypeScript community plays a significant role in the language's development. Participating in the community by reporting issues, contributing to discussions, and sharing your experiences can help shape the future of TypeScript. It also provides opportunities to learn from others and stay informed about upcoming changes.

GitHub discussions, forums, and social media platforms are great places to engage with the TypeScript community and share your insights.

7. Consider a TypeScript Version Manager

If your project relies on multiple TypeScript versions simultaneously, consider using a TypeScript version manager like tsup or nvm (Node Version Manager). These tools allow you to switch between different TypeScript versions for different projects or parts of your codebase, providing flexibility and compatibility when dealing with updates.

In conclusion, staying prepared for future TypeScript updates is crucial for maintaining the health and longevity of your projects. By keeping dependencies up-to-date, monitoring release notes, testing your code, and actively engaging with the TypeScript community, you can ensure a smooth transition to newer versions and continue to leverage the power of TypeScript in your development endeavors.

Section 20.5: Conclusion: The Ongoing Journey from JavaScript to TypeScript

In this concluding section, we reflect on the journey from JavaScript to TypeScript and discuss the significance of TypeScript in the world of web development. TypeScript has emerged as a powerful and widely adopted language that offers a safer and more productive way to write JavaScript applications. As we wrap up this book, it's essential to emphasize key takeaways and the role TypeScript plays in the ever-evolving landscape of web development.

1. The Power of Static Typing

TypeScript's static typing brings immense benefits to developers. It enables early error detection, improved code quality, enhanced tooling support, and better collaboration within development teams. By catching type-related issues at compile-time, TypeScript reduces the likelihood of runtime errors, making code more robust and maintainable.

2. Evolving JavaScript Ecosystem

JavaScript is continually evolving, and TypeScript evolves with it. As new JavaScript features and standards are introduced, TypeScript incorporates them, providing developers with access to the latest language capabilities while maintaining backward compatibility. TypeScript's ability to adapt to the changing JavaScript landscape ensures that developers can stay up-to-date with modern web development practices.

3. Strong Tooling and IDE Support

TypeScript's ecosystem includes a rich set of development tools and IDE integrations that enhance the development experience. Popular code editors like Visual Studio Code offer excellent TypeScript support, including features such as intelligent code completion, automatic refactoring, and real-time error checking. This tooling empowers developers to write clean and efficient code more quickly.

4. Community and Open Source

The TypeScript community has grown significantly over the years. Developers worldwide contribute to TypeScript's development, create libraries and frameworks, and share knowledge through forums, blogs, and social media. This collaborative spirit has been instrumental in TypeScript's success and ensures a bright future for the language.

5. Versatility Across Domains

TypeScript's versatility extends beyond web development. It has found applications in backend development, mobile app development, game development, IoT, and more. Its ability to target multiple platforms and environments makes it a valuable choice for a wide range of projects.

6. Preparing for the Future

As we discussed in the previous section, preparing for future TypeScript updates is essential. TypeScript's commitment to staying up-to-date with JavaScript standards and addressing developer needs ensures its relevance in the years to come. Developers should embrace best practices for managing dependencies, monitoring TypeScript release notes, and actively participating in the TypeScript community to stay informed and ready for future changes.

7. Conclusion

In conclusion, TypeScript has come a long way since its inception, and it has established itself as a fundamental tool for modern web development. Its static typing, robust tooling, adaptability, and strong community support make it a valuable asset for developers and organizations alike. As the JavaScript ecosystem continues to evolve, TypeScript remains a reliable choice for building scalable, maintainable, and error-free applications.

We hope this book has provided you with a comprehensive understanding of TypeScript and its various applications. Whether you're a frontend developer, a backend engineer, or a mobile app developer, TypeScript has something valuable to offer. As you embark on your journey with TypeScript, remember that learning and adapting are key to becoming a proficient TypeScript developer. Embrace the opportunities it brings, and enjoy the benefits of writing safer and more maintainable code in the exciting world of web development.